Inside the World of Bill Joy

The BSD and Java Visionary – Unofficial

Mei Nascimento

ISBN: 9781779699909
Imprint: Telephasic Workshop
Copyright © 2024 Mei Nascimento.
All Rights Reserved.

Contents

Introduction: Who the Fuck Is Bill Joy?   1
The Godfather of Open-Source Software: How Bill Joy Became a Tech Fucking Visionary   1

The Fucking Early Years: Creating BSD at Berkeley   15
The Birth of BSD: How Bill Joy Took on AT&T and Unix   15
Bill Joy's Fucking Impact on the Open-Source Community   28

Sun Microsystems and the Creation of Java   41
From Berkeley to Sun: How Bill Joy Made His Fucking Mark on Silicon Valley   41
The Fucking Birth of Java: Changing the Internet Forever   54

Bill Joy's Fucking Leadership Style and Vision   67
The Fucking Genius and the Perfectionist: Bill Joy's Approach to Innovation   67
The Fucking Power of Vision   79

The Fucking Personal Cost of Revolutionizing Technology   93
The Fucking Pressure of Leading the Tech Fucking World   93
Reflections on Joy's Fucking Career and Legacy   104

Index   117

Introduction: Who the Fuck Is Bill Joy?

The Godfather of Open-Source Software: How Bill Joy Became a Tech Fucking Visionary

From Berkeley to Sun Microsystems: The Fucking Journey of a Programming Genius

Bill Joy's journey from the hallowed halls of the University of California, Berkeley, to the bustling offices of Sun Microsystems is nothing short of legendary. It is a tale of intellect, innovation, and an unyielding spirit that reshaped the very fabric of computing. This section dives deep into the milestones of Joy's career, exploring the pivotal moments that defined his path and the impact of his work on the tech world.

The Berkeley Breakthrough

In the late 1970s, Joy was a graduate student at Berkeley, where he was immersed in the world of computer science. It was here that he encountered the AT&T Unix operating system, which was both revolutionary and restrictive. Joy quickly recognized the potential of Unix but also its limitations due to licensing issues. Determined to create a more accessible version, Joy spearheaded the Berkeley Software Distribution (BSD) project.

The BSD project was not just about software; it was a statement against the corporate mentality that sought to restrict access to technology. Joy and his team at Berkeley innovated by adding features that made BSD not only a viable alternative to Unix but a superior one. They introduced networking capabilities that allowed multiple computers to communicate seamlessly, which was groundbreaking at the time. This innovation laid the groundwork for what would eventually become the Internet as we know it.

$$\text{Networking Efficiency} = \frac{\text{Data Transferred}}{\text{Time Taken}} \quad \text{(measured in Mbps)} \qquad (1)$$

The above equation illustrates the importance of efficiency in networking, a principle that Joy and his team prioritized. Their work in developing TCP/IP protocols within BSD was instrumental in establishing standards that are still in use today.

The Transition to Sun Microsystems

In 1982, Joy's journey took a significant turn when he co-founded Sun Microsystems. The company was born out of a vision to create workstations that could harness the power of Unix while being more accessible to developers. Joy's experience with BSD played a crucial role in shaping Sun's product line.

At Sun, Joy faced the challenge of translating his academic innovations into commercial products. This transition was not without its difficulties. The tech landscape was rapidly evolving, and Joy had to navigate the complex interplay between innovation and market demands. His leadership style, characterized by a relentless pursuit of perfection, became a cornerstone of Sun's culture.

Innovative Products and Challenges

One of the first products that emerged from Sun was the Sun-1 workstation, which was notable for its use of the BSD operating system. Joy's vision was clear: to create a machine that could run software efficiently and effectively. The Sun-1 was a massive success, and it set the stage for subsequent models that would dominate the market.

However, the road was not always smooth. Joy encountered significant challenges, including competition from established players like IBM and the ever-evolving landscape of technology. The need to innovate constantly meant that Joy had to push his team to their limits, balancing the drive for groundbreaking technology with the realities of business.

$$\text{Innovation Index} = \frac{\text{Number of New Features}}{\text{Time to Market}} \quad \text{(measured in features/month)} \qquad (2)$$

This equation underscores the importance of rapid innovation in the tech industry, a principle that Joy embraced wholeheartedly. His ability to foster a culture of creativity and risk-taking was instrumental in Sun's success.

Legacy and Influence

Joy's journey from Berkeley to Sun Microsystems is not just a personal story; it is a narrative that reflects the evolution of the tech industry itself. His contributions to BSD and the establishment of Sun Microsystems laid the groundwork for modern computing. The open-source philosophy that Joy championed became a guiding principle for countless developers and companies.

Today, the influence of Joy's work is evident in the very fabric of the software industry. The principles of open-source software, collaboration, and innovation that he advocated continue to resonate with new generations of programmers. His legacy is not just in the code he wrote but in the ethos he instilled in the tech community.

As we look to the future, it is clear that Bill Joy's journey is far from over. His vision for a world where technology is accessible and collaborative remains a driving force in the industry. The lessons learned from his experiences at Berkeley and Sun Microsystems serve as a reminder that the journey of a programming genius is one of constant evolution and relentless pursuit of excellence.

Conclusion

In conclusion, the journey of Bill Joy from Berkeley to Sun Microsystems exemplifies the power of vision, creativity, and determination. His contributions have not only shaped the landscape of computing but have also inspired countless individuals to pursue their passions in technology. As we continue to navigate the complexities of the digital age, Joy's legacy serves as a beacon of innovation and a testament to the impact one individual can have on the world.

The Creation of BSD: Why Bill Joy's Fucking Legacy Changed the World of Operating Systems

In the late 1970s, the computing landscape was dominated by proprietary systems, particularly AT&T's Unix, which was a closed-source behemoth that restricted access to its source code. Enter Bill Joy, a programming prodigy whose vision would not only challenge the status quo but also lay the foundation for a revolution in operating systems. This section explores how Joy's creation of the Berkeley Software Distribution (BSD) fundamentally altered the trajectory of software development and established a legacy that resonates to this day.

The Context of BSD's Creation

To understand the significance of BSD, we must first grasp the limitations imposed by closed-source software. AT&T's Unix was a powerful system, but it was shrouded in secrecy and restrictive licensing agreements. This environment stifled innovation and collaboration, leading to a fragmented ecosystem where developers were often forced to work in isolation. Joy, along with his team at the University of California, Berkeley, recognized that the future of computing lay in collaboration and openness.

The Breakthrough: BSD

In 1977, Joy and his colleagues embarked on a mission to create a version of Unix that was not only accessible but also enhanced. This initiative culminated in the release of the first Berkeley Software Distribution (BSD) in 1978. BSD was groundbreaking for several reasons:

- **Open Access:** For the first time, universities and developers had access to the source code of an operating system, allowing them to modify and improve it freely. This openness laid the groundwork for a collaborative approach to software development.

- **Enhanced Features:** BSD introduced numerous enhancements over traditional Unix, including the first implementation of the TCP/IP networking protocols, which would become the backbone of the Internet. This was no small feat; the integration of networking capabilities into the operating system fundamentally changed how computers communicated.

- **User-Friendly Tools:** Joy's team developed a suite of user-friendly tools and utilities that made BSD more accessible to users. This included the vi text editor, which remains popular among programmers to this day.

The Philosophical Shift: Open Source

Joy's work on BSD was not merely technical; it represented a philosophical shift in the software community. He believed that software should be free, both in terms of cost and accessibility. This belief was articulated in his famous quote, "Good software, like wine, takes time." This perspective not only championed the idea of open-source software but also inspired a generation of developers to prioritize collaboration over competition.

Case Studies: Key Breakthroughs in BSD

Several key breakthroughs emerged from the BSD project that exemplify Joy's impact:

1. **Networking Innovations:** The inclusion of TCP/IP protocols in BSD was a game-changer. It allowed disparate systems to communicate over the nascent Internet, paving the way for the interconnected world we know today. The adoption of these protocols by other operating systems solidified BSD's role as a foundational technology.

2. **File System Improvements:** BSD introduced the Fast File System (FFS), which optimized disk performance and reliability. The FFS was a significant advancement that influenced later file systems, including those used in Linux and macOS.

3. **Development Environment:** BSD provided a robust development environment that encouraged experimentation. This led to the creation of several programming languages and tools, including the C programming language, which Joy himself had a hand in popularizing.

The Legacy of BSD

The impact of BSD extends far beyond its immediate success. It served as the foundation for many modern operating systems, including FreeBSD, NetBSD, and OpenBSD, which continue to thrive in various applications today. Moreover, the principles of open-source software that Joy championed have become a cornerstone of modern software development, leading to the rise of collaborative platforms like GitHub and the Linux operating system.

Conclusion: Bill Joy's Lasting Influence

In summary, Bill Joy's creation of BSD was not just a technical achievement; it was a revolutionary act that transformed the landscape of operating systems and set the stage for the open-source movement. His legacy is a testament to the power of collaboration, innovation, and the belief that software should be free for all. As we continue to navigate the complexities of modern computing, Joy's vision remains a guiding light, reminding us that the best solutions often arise from shared knowledge and collective effort.

$$\text{Impact}_{BSD} = \text{Open Access} + \text{Networking Innovations} + \text{User-Friendly Tools} \tag{3}$$

This equation encapsulates the essence of Joy's contributions, illustrating how the combination of open access, innovative networking, and usability transformed the world of operating systems forever. The legacy of Bill Joy is indeed a fucking monumental one, altering not just the course of technology but also the very philosophy of how we approach software development.

Java's Architect: How Bill Joy's Fucking Influence Helped Shape the Future of the Internet

Bill Joy, often hailed as a programming prodigy, played a pivotal role in shaping Java, a language that would become synonymous with the Internet revolution. As the architect of many foundational technologies, Joy's influence on Java was not merely a footnote in history but a defining moment that set the stage for the future of web development. This section delves into how Joy's vision and technical prowess contributed to the creation of Java, ensuring its place as a cornerstone of modern computing.

The Vision Behind Java

The inception of Java in the mid-1990s was driven by the need for a programming language that could operate seamlessly across various platforms. Joy recognized that the future of computing lay in the ability to create software that transcended hardware limitations. This foresight was encapsulated in the mantra: "Write Once, Run Anywhere" (WORA). The core philosophy behind this principle was that Java should be able to run on any device that had a Java Virtual Machine (JVM), thus eliminating the barriers imposed by different operating systems.

The theoretical underpinning of WORA can be expressed in the following equation:

$$\text{Platform Independence} = \frac{\text{Source Code}}{\text{JVM}} \tag{4}$$

Where the source code is the Java program written by developers, and the JVM serves as the intermediary that allows execution on any platform. This abstraction layer was crucial in enabling developers to focus on writing code without worrying about the underlying hardware specifics.

Technical Innovations and Challenges

Creating a language that could achieve platform independence was fraught with challenges. One of the significant innovations introduced by Joy and his team was the concept of bytecode. Instead of compiling Java code directly into machine code, Java compilers translate source code into an intermediate form known as bytecode. This bytecode is then interpreted or compiled just-in-time (JIT) by the JVM, allowing it to run on any device that supports Java.

The equation that represents the compilation process can be summarized as follows:

$$\text{Java Source Code} \xrightarrow{\text{Java Compiler}} \text{Bytecode} \xrightarrow{\text{JVM}} \text{Machine Code} \quad (5)$$

This innovation not only facilitated portability but also enhanced security by providing an additional layer of abstraction. The JVM acts as a sandbox, executing bytecode in a controlled environment, which mitigates the risks associated with running potentially malicious code.

However, the journey was not without its hurdles. The initial performance of Java applications was often criticized compared to natively compiled languages like C or C++. Joy's team had to overcome these performance bottlenecks through various optimizations in the JVM, including adaptive optimization techniques that allowed the JVM to improve the execution speed of frequently run code segments dynamically.

Case Studies: Java's Impact on Web Development

Java's introduction was a game-changer for web development. The emergence of applets—small Java programs that could be embedded in web pages—revolutionized the way users interacted with the web. Although applets eventually fell out of favor due to security concerns and the rise of other technologies, they laid the groundwork for more dynamic web applications.

One of the most significant impacts of Java was the creation of JavaServer Pages (JSP) and Servlets, which enabled developers to create dynamic web content. This shift from static HTML pages to dynamic web applications was crucial for the evolution of the Internet as we know it today.

The equation representing the transformation of web applications can be expressed as:

$$\text{Static HTML} \xrightarrow{\text{Java}} \text{Dynamic Web Applications} \quad (6)$$

This dynamic capability allowed for interactive features, user authentication, and database connectivity, which became essential components of modern web applications.

The Legacy of Bill Joy in Java Development

Joy's contributions to Java extended beyond its technical specifications; his philosophy regarding open-source development and community engagement helped foster a vibrant ecosystem around the language. Joy believed that programming knowledge should be shared, and this ethos was reflected in Java's licensing model, which encouraged widespread adoption and collaboration.

The influence of Joy's vision can still be felt today. Java remains one of the most widely used programming languages globally, powering everything from enterprise applications to mobile devices. The community that has grown around Java continues to innovate, furthering Joy's legacy of open-source collaboration and technological advancement.

Conclusion: The Future of Java and Its Ongoing Relevance

As we look to the future, the relevance of Java in the ever-evolving landscape of technology cannot be overstated. Bill Joy's influence as a visionary architect of Java laid the foundation for a language that continues to adapt and thrive in the face of new challenges. With the rise of cloud computing, big data, and artificial intelligence, Java's versatility and robustness ensure its place in the next generation of technological advancements.

In summary, Bill Joy's fucking influence on Java was not just about creating a programming language; it was about envisioning a future where software could break free from hardware constraints, democratizing access to technology and empowering developers worldwide. As we navigate the complexities of modern computing, Joy's legacy serves as both an inspiration and a guiding principle for future innovations in the tech industry.

The Importance of Open-Source Fucking Philosophy: Why Bill Joy Believed Software Should Be Free

Bill Joy, a name synonymous with groundbreaking advancements in computing, was not just a programming genius but also a staunch advocate for the open-source philosophy. This section delves into the importance of this philosophy in Joy's work and why he believed that software should be free, both in spirit and in practice.

The Philosophy of Open Source

At its core, the open-source philosophy advocates for the free distribution and access to software source code. Joy's belief stemmed from the idea that collaboration and transparency lead to innovation, a notion that can be traced back to the early days of computing. In the 1970s and 1980s, when Joy was making his mark, the tech landscape was dominated by proprietary software, often locked away behind corporate walls. Joy recognized that this approach stifled creativity and hindered progress.

> "The software industry is a lot like the music industry. If you lock your music away, it won't evolve. If you share it, it becomes a living, breathing entity that grows and adapts."

Joy's vision was that software should be a communal resource, accessible to all. He famously asserted that *"the future is open"*, a mantra that resonated with many developers who sought to break free from the constraints of closed systems.

The Impact of BSD

The Berkeley Software Distribution (BSD) is a prime example of Joy's commitment to open-source principles. Developed at the University of California, Berkeley, BSD was not just a Unix variant; it was a platform for innovation. Joy and his team made significant contributions to networking and file systems, which were released under permissive licenses. This allowed other developers to build upon their work without the fear of legal repercussions.

The impact of BSD on the open-source community cannot be overstated. It laid the groundwork for Linux and inspired a generation of programmers to embrace the idea of sharing code. This was a radical departure from the corporate mentality of the time, which viewed software as a proprietary asset rather than a collaborative effort.

The Open-Source Movement and Its Challenges

Despite the benefits of open-source software, Joy faced significant challenges in advocating for this philosophy. The corporate world was resistant to change, often viewing open-source as a threat to their business models. Companies like Microsoft, which thrived on proprietary software, pushed back against the idea of free software, arguing that it undermined intellectual property rights.

Joy countered this argument by emphasizing the long-term benefits of open-source software. He believed that when developers share their work, they create a richer ecosystem that ultimately benefits everyone. This is encapsulated in the equation:

$$\text{Innovation} = \text{Collaboration} + \text{Transparency} \qquad (7)$$

In this equation, Joy posited that innovation is directly proportional to the levels of collaboration and transparency in the software development process. The more developers collaborate and share their code, the greater the potential for groundbreaking advancements.

Case Studies in Open Source

Several case studies illustrate Joy's impact on the open-source movement. One notable example is the rise of the Apache web server, which became the most widely used web server software in the world. The collaborative nature of its development, rooted in the open-source philosophy, allowed it to adapt quickly to the needs of users and developers alike.

Another example is the emergence of the Linux operating system, which owes much of its success to the principles championed by Joy. Linus Torvalds, the creator of Linux, was inspired by the open-source movement that Joy helped to popularize. The collaborative development model of Linux has led to a robust ecosystem of distributions, each tailored to different user needs.

The Future of Open Source

As we look to the future, Joy's vision for open-source software remains relevant. The tech landscape is evolving, with new challenges such as cybersecurity and data privacy emerging. Open-source software offers a solution to these challenges by promoting transparency and community-driven development.

Joy's assertion that *"software should be free"* is not just about cost; it's about freedom of choice, innovation, and collaboration. The open-source movement has proven that when developers come together, they can create solutions that are not only effective but also equitable.

In conclusion, Bill Joy's belief in the importance of open-source philosophy has left an indelible mark on the software industry. His legacy continues to inspire developers to share their knowledge and collaborate for the greater good, ensuring that the future of computing remains open and accessible for all. The journey of open-source software is far from over, and as Joy himself might say, *"Let's keep it fucking free!"*

The Future of Computing: How Joy's Fucking Vision Continues to Shape Tech Development

Bill Joy, a name synonymous with groundbreaking innovation, has left an indelible mark on the world of technology. His vision, which championed open-source software and emphasized the importance of collaboration, continues to resonate in today's tech landscape. This section delves into how Joy's philosophy and contributions are shaping the future of computing, addressing relevant theories, ongoing challenges, and real-world examples that illustrate his enduring influence.

The Open-Source Movement: A Legacy of Collaboration

At the heart of Joy's vision lies the open-source philosophy, which posits that software should be freely accessible and modifiable by anyone. This principle has fueled a revolution in software development, fostering a collaborative environment where developers across the globe can contribute to and improve upon existing code. The impact of this movement is palpable in projects like `Linux`, `Apache`, and `Kubernetes`, which have become foundational to modern computing infrastructure.

The success of these projects can be attributed to the very essence of Joy's philosophy: *"Innovation thrives in an open environment."* By allowing developers to share knowledge and resources, the open-source movement has accelerated technological advancement and democratized access to powerful tools. In 2020, the `Linux` operating system was reported to run on over 70% of cloud infrastructure, a testament to the effectiveness of Joy's vision.

The Rise of Cloud Computing and Distributed Systems

Joy's foresight into the future of computing can also be seen in the rise of cloud computing and distributed systems. As he once predicted, the ability to access computing resources over the internet has transformed how businesses operate. This shift towards cloud-based solutions allows for scalability, flexibility, and cost-effectiveness, enabling organizations to adapt to changing demands rapidly.

The equation governing the efficiency of cloud computing can be represented as:

$$E = \frac{C}{R} \qquad (8)$$

where E represents efficiency, C is the total computing cost, and R is the resources utilized. Joy's emphasis on efficient resource management is exemplified by the widespread adoption of cloud services like `Amazon Web Services` (AWS) and `Microsoft Azure`, which leverage distributed systems to provide on-demand computing power.

Artificial Intelligence: The Next Frontier

Another domain where Joy's influence is evident is artificial intelligence (AI). His belief in the power of computing to solve complex problems has paved the way for advancements in machine learning and AI technologies. Joy's early work on BSD and his contributions to programming languages laid the groundwork for the development of algorithms that drive AI today.

However, the rapid evolution of AI also presents ethical challenges that Joy's vision can help address. As AI systems become more integrated into society, questions surrounding bias, transparency, and accountability have emerged. Joy's advocacy for open-source principles can guide the development of ethical AI frameworks, ensuring that these technologies are built with fairness and inclusivity in mind.

For example, the `Fairness, Accountability, and Transparency in Machine Learning` (FAT/ML) initiative reflects Joy's commitment to collaborative problem-solving. By bringing together researchers and practitioners from diverse backgrounds, this initiative seeks to establish guidelines that promote ethical practices in AI development.

The Internet of Things (IoT): Connecting the World

Joy's vision also extends to the Internet of Things (IoT), where interconnected devices are reshaping our daily lives. The proliferation of smart devices, from home assistants to industrial sensors, exemplifies the potential of Joy's ideas to create a more connected world. The framework for IoT can be modeled using the equation:

$$D = N \cdot C \tag{9}$$

where D is the total number of devices, N represents the number of networks, and C is the connectivity per device. Joy's contributions to networking and protocol development have enabled seamless communication between devices, driving the growth of IoT applications across various sectors.

However, the rapid expansion of IoT also brings challenges related to security and privacy. Joy's advocacy for open-source development can provide solutions to these issues by promoting transparency in device design and encouraging community-driven security practices.

The Future of Programming Languages

Finally, Joy's impact on programming languages cannot be overstated. As the architect of Java, he envisioned a language that could run on any platform, a concept that has become increasingly relevant in today's multi-platform environment. The principles of platform independence and ease of use are now foundational in languages like Python and Go, which are widely adopted for their versatility and developer-friendly syntax.

The evolution of programming languages can be summarized by the equation:

$$P = U + A \qquad (10)$$

where P represents the programming language's popularity, U is usability, and A is adaptability. Joy's emphasis on creating languages that prioritize these factors continues to inspire language design and development, ensuring that future programming languages remain accessible and effective.

Conclusion: A Vision for the Future

In conclusion, Bill Joy's vision continues to shape the future of computing in profound ways. His advocacy for open-source software, foresight into cloud computing, contributions to AI, insights into IoT, and influence on programming languages have laid a robust foundation for ongoing innovation. As we navigate the complexities of modern technology, Joy's principles serve as a guiding light, reminding us that collaboration, transparency, and inclusivity are essential for creating a better, more connected world. The future of computing is bright, and it is built on the legacy of a man who dared to dream big and share his vision with the world.

The Fucking Early Years: Creating BSD at Berkeley

The Birth of BSD: How Bill Joy Took on AT&T and Unix

Fucking Innovating at Berkeley: How Joy Led the Team that Made BSD a Fucking Powerhouse

In the late 1970s, the University of California, Berkeley, became a hotbed of innovation in the realm of computing, largely due to the relentless efforts of Bill Joy and his team. The genesis of the Berkeley Software Distribution (BSD) was not just a technical endeavor; it was a revolution that challenged the status quo of proprietary software and set the stage for the open-source movement.

The Context of Innovation

At that time, Unix was the predominant operating system, developed by AT&T. However, it was costly and restrictive, often leaving users frustrated with its limitations. Joy, with a vision that transcended conventional boundaries, saw an opportunity to create a version of Unix that was not only free but also enriched with enhancements that would make it more robust and versatile.

The initial challenge was to obtain the source code for Unix, which was tightly controlled by AT&T. Joy and his team managed to reverse-engineer the operating system, gaining insights into its architecture and functionality. This act of defiance was not merely an act of rebellion; it was a demonstration of Joy's belief that software should be open and accessible to all.

The Team Dynamics

Joy assembled a team of brilliant minds at Berkeley, including notable figures such as Mike Karels, Marshall Kirk McKusick, and others who shared his passion for innovation. Together, they fostered a culture of collaboration and creativity, which became the bedrock of their success.

The team utilized a unique approach to problem-solving, often employing iterative development methods that allowed for rapid prototyping and testing. This methodology was critical in addressing the myriad of issues that arose during the development of BSD.

Key Innovations in BSD

One of the most significant contributions of Joy and his team was the development of the TCP/IP networking protocols, which were integrated into BSD. This was a game-changer, as it enabled BSD to communicate over networks, laying the groundwork for the modern Internet. The implementation of these protocols is often summarized by the equation:

$$\text{TCP/IP} = \text{Transmission Control Protocol} + \text{Internet Protocol} \quad (11)$$

This innovation not only enhanced BSD's capabilities but also positioned it as a leading contender against Unix, demonstrating its potential for scalability and flexibility.

Another major breakthrough was the introduction of the virtual memory system in BSD. This system allowed multiple processes to run simultaneously, each with its own memory space, significantly improving the efficiency of resource utilization. The theoretical foundation behind virtual memory can be expressed as:

$$\text{Virtual Memory} = \frac{\text{Physical Memory}}{\text{Process Isolation}} \quad (12)$$

This concept of isolation was crucial for security and stability, allowing users to run applications without the fear of crashing the entire system.

Case Studies of Success

The success of BSD can be illustrated through several case studies that highlight its impact on both academia and industry. For instance, the integration of the vi text editor, developed by Joy himself, became a staple in the Unix community. Its efficiency and power made it the go-to tool for programmers, illustrating how user-centric design can drive adoption.

Additionally, BSD's influence on the development of the Internet cannot be overstated. As more universities and research institutions adopted BSD, the network grew exponentially, leading to a collaborative environment that fostered innovation across various domains.

Challenges Faced

Despite the successes, Joy and his team faced numerous challenges, particularly from AT&T, which sought to protect its intellectual property. The legal battles over the rights to Unix code were fierce, yet Joy remained steadfast in his commitment to open-source principles.

The tension between innovation and corporate interests created a high-stakes environment, but it also galvanized the team to push forward with their mission. Joy's leadership style, characterized by a blend of technical prowess and visionary thinking, inspired his team to navigate these challenges with determination.

Conclusion

In conclusion, Bill Joy's leadership at Berkeley was instrumental in transforming BSD into a powerhouse of innovation. By fostering a collaborative environment, embracing open-source principles, and tackling the challenges head-on, Joy and his team not only created a powerful operating system but also laid the foundation for the future of computing. The legacy of BSD continues to resonate in the open-source community, reminding us that the spirit of innovation thrives when knowledge is shared and collaboration is encouraged.

The journey of BSD is a testament to the power of visionary leadership and the relentless pursuit of excellence in the face of adversity. As we reflect on Joy's contributions, it becomes clear that his impact on technology will endure for generations to come.

Case Studies: The Fucking Key Breakthroughs That Made BSD a Fucking Competitor to Unix

In the rapidly evolving landscape of computing during the late 1970s and early 1980s, the Berkeley Software Distribution (BSD) emerged as a formidable contender against the established Unix operating system. Bill Joy, with his indomitable spirit and relentless innovation, spearheaded several breakthroughs that not only challenged Unix's dominance but also set the stage for modern operating systems. This section delves into the key advancements that made BSD a fucking competitor to Unix.

The Fucking TCP/IP Stack

One of the most significant breakthroughs in BSD was the integration of the Transmission Control Protocol/Internet Protocol (TCP/IP) stack. In the early days of networking, Unix systems primarily utilized proprietary networking protocols, limiting their interoperability. Joy and his team at Berkeley recognized the growing importance of networking and championed the adoption of TCP/IP as a standard.

$$TCP/IP = TCP + IP \qquad (13)$$

Where: - TCP (Transmission Control Protocol) ensures reliable transmission of data. - IP (Internet Protocol) handles addressing and routing of packets.

This integration not only enabled BSD to communicate effectively over the burgeoning internet but also positioned it as a precursor to the modern networking standards we rely on today. The inclusion of TCP/IP in BSD was revolutionary, as it allowed diverse systems to connect seamlessly, paving the way for the internet's explosive growth.

The Fucking Virtual Memory System

Another groundbreaking advancement was the implementation of a virtual memory system in BSD. Traditional Unix systems operated with fixed memory allocation, which often led to inefficient use of resources and limited the scalability of applications. Bill Joy and his team devised a virtual memory system that allowed processes to use more memory than was physically available, effectively utilizing disk space as an extension of RAM.

The fundamental concept can be summarized as follows:

$$\text{Virtual Memory} = \text{Physical Memory} + \text{Disk Space} \qquad (14)$$

This innovation allowed multiple processes to run concurrently without exhausting physical memory, thus enhancing the performance and responsiveness of applications. The virtual memory system became a cornerstone of modern operating systems, influencing subsequent designs in both BSD and other Unix-like systems.

The Fucking File System Enhancements

BSD also introduced significant enhancements to the file system, most notably the Fast File System (FFS). Traditional Unix file systems suffered from performance bottlenecks, particularly with large files and directories. Joy's team restructured the file system to improve access times and reliability.

The key features of the Fast File System included:

- **Block Grouping:** FFS organized data into block groups, reducing seek times and improving read/write performance.

- **Fragmentation Management:** By managing disk fragmentation more effectively, FFS minimized the performance degradation associated with scattered data.

- **Improved Caching:** FFS utilized advanced caching techniques to speed up file access, significantly boosting overall system performance.

These enhancements made BSD's file system not only faster but also more robust, allowing it to handle larger datasets and more complex file operations than its Unix counterparts.

The Fucking Development Environment

Another critical breakthrough was the development of a rich programming environment within BSD. Recognizing the importance of a robust development ecosystem, Joy and his team integrated various tools that facilitated software development, including the vi text editor, the make build automation tool, and the gcc compiler.

The integration of these tools created a cohesive environment that empowered developers to write, compile, and debug code efficiently. This environment became a breeding ground for innovation, as programmers could rapidly prototype and deploy applications, significantly contributing to the growth of the open-source community.

The Fucking Community and Documentation

Finally, BSD's success can be attributed to the vibrant community and comprehensive documentation that surrounded it. Bill Joy understood that for BSD to compete with Unix, it needed a dedicated user base and accessible resources. The BSD community fostered collaboration and knowledge sharing, which was crucial for its growth.

The documentation provided by the community was extensive, covering everything from installation procedures to advanced system administration. This emphasis on community support and documentation ensured that users could effectively utilize BSD, further solidifying its position as a serious competitor to Unix.

Conclusion

In conclusion, the key breakthroughs that made BSD a fucking competitor to Unix were not merely technological advancements but also philosophical shifts in how software was developed and shared. The integration of TCP/IP, the implementation of virtual memory, enhancements to the file system, the creation of a robust development environment, and the fostering of a supportive community all contributed to BSD's legacy. Bill Joy's vision and relentless pursuit of innovation transformed BSD from a mere derivative of Unix into a powerful operating system that laid the groundwork for the open-source movement and continues to influence modern computing. The impact of these breakthroughs reverberates through the tech industry, reminding us of the importance of collaboration, innovation, and the belief that software should be free and accessible to all.

The Fucking Open-Source Battle: How Bill Joy Fought to Keep Software Free and Open for Everyone

In the late 1970s and early 1980s, as the tech world was rapidly evolving, a fierce ideological battle began to brew—one that would shape the future of software development and the very essence of programming culture. At the forefront of this battle was Bill Joy, a figure whose contributions to the field were as profound as they were controversial. Joy's commitment to the open-source philosophy was not merely a personal belief; it was a rallying cry against the corporate greed that threatened to stifle innovation and limit access to technology.

The Context of the Open-Source Movement

To understand the stakes of this battle, one must first grasp the landscape of software distribution in the late 20th century. The dominant paradigm was that of proprietary software, where companies like Microsoft and IBM held tight control over their code. Users were often required to purchase licenses that came with restrictions, preventing them from modifying or sharing the software. This model not only limited the potential for innovation but also created a culture of secrecy that stifled collaboration.

In contrast, Joy and his contemporaries at Berkeley believed that knowledge should be shared, not hoarded. The ethos of the open-source movement was born from the idea that collaboration leads to better software, as developers could build upon each other's work. Joy famously stated, "The best way to predict the future is to invent it," embodying a philosophy that encouraged experimentation and communal effort.

The Birth of BSD and the Fight Against AT&T

Joy's pivotal role in the development of the Berkeley Software Distribution (BSD) was a direct response to the restrictive licensing practices of AT&T, the owner of Unix. In the early days, Unix was a powerful operating system, but access to its source code was tightly controlled. Joy and his team at Berkeley sought to create a version of Unix that was accessible to everyone, free from the shackles of corporate licensing.

The initial challenge was formidable. Joy and his colleagues faced legal threats from AT&T, which sought to protect its intellectual property. However, Joy was undeterred. He understood that the future of computing depended on making software freely available. In a bold move, he and his team decided to release BSD under a permissive license, allowing anyone to use, modify, and distribute the software.

This decision was not just a technical achievement; it was a declaration of war against the corporate mentality that sought to control the flow of information. Joy's actions demonstrated that software could be a communal resource, and this notion resonated deeply within the burgeoning tech community.

The Impact of BSD on the Open-Source Movement

The release of BSD had far-reaching implications. It not only provided a robust alternative to proprietary Unix but also laid the groundwork for the open-source movement that would follow. Developers from around the world began to contribute to BSD, improving its functionality and expanding its reach. This collaborative effort exemplified the power of open-source software: when individuals come together to share knowledge, the results can be nothing short of revolutionary.

One of the most significant outcomes of this movement was the eventual emergence of Linux, which drew heavily from the principles established by BSD. Linus Torvalds, the creator of Linux, cited Joy's work as an inspiration, highlighting the importance of free software in fostering innovation. The open-source battle that Joy fought was not just about one operating system; it was about creating a culture of openness that would empower generations of developers.

The Philosophical Beliefs Behind Open Source

At the heart of Joy's advocacy for open-source software lay a set of philosophical beliefs that transcended mere technical considerations. He argued that programming knowledge should be democratized, accessible to anyone with the curiosity and drive to learn. This perspective was rooted in the belief that technology should serve humanity, rather than be controlled by a select few.

Joy's philosophy can be encapsulated in the following equation:

$$\text{Innovation} = \text{Collaboration} + \text{Freedom}$$

This equation underscores the idea that true innovation arises when individuals are free to collaborate and share their ideas without fear of retribution or restriction. Joy believed that when developers are empowered to work together, the entire tech ecosystem benefits, leading to advancements that can change the world.

Challenges and Resistance

Despite the successes of the open-source movement, Joy faced significant resistance from corporate interests who viewed open-source software as a threat to their profitability. Companies invested heavily in proprietary models and were reluctant to embrace the notion of free software. Joy's battle was not just against legal threats but also against a prevailing mindset that prioritized profit over progress.

In response, Joy and other open-source advocates organized conferences, wrote articles, and engaged in public speaking to raise awareness about the benefits of open-source software. They emphasized that open-source projects could lead to higher quality software, reduced costs, and increased security—benefits that could not be ignored by businesses.

Legacy and the Future of Open Source

Today, the legacy of Bill Joy's fight for open-source software is evident in the thriving ecosystems of projects like Linux, Apache, and countless others. Joy's vision has inspired a new generation of developers who continue to champion the principles of openness and collaboration. The open-source model has become a cornerstone of modern software development, with major companies like Google and Facebook contributing to open-source projects.

As we look to the future, the question remains: will the spirit of open-source continue to thrive in an increasingly corporate world? Joy's battle laid the foundation for a movement that is now more relevant than ever. The ongoing fight for free and open software is not just about code; it's about ensuring that technology remains a tool for empowerment rather than a means of control.

In conclusion, Bill Joy's relentless pursuit of open-source principles transformed the tech landscape and inspired a movement that champions freedom, collaboration, and innovation. His legacy serves as a reminder that the fight for open access to knowledge is an ongoing battle—one that requires passion, dedication, and a willingness to challenge the status quo. As we navigate the complexities of modern technology, Joy's vision continues to illuminate the path forward, ensuring that software remains free and open for everyone.

The Fucking Innovations in Networking and File Systems That Made BSD Stand Out

The Berkeley Software Distribution (BSD) operating system is not just a mere fork of Unix; it is a revolutionary platform that introduced groundbreaking innovations in networking and file systems. Bill Joy and his team at the University of California, Berkeley, were not only focused on making an operating system that functioned well but were also determined to push the boundaries of what was possible in computing. This section delves into the fucking innovations that made BSD a standout choice for developers and organizations alike.

Networking Innovations: The TCP/IP Stack

One of the most significant contributions of BSD to the computing world was its implementation of the Transmission Control Protocol/Internet Protocol (TCP/IP) stack. In the early 1980s, the Internet was a nascent concept, and networking protocols were still being developed. Joy recognized the potential of networked computing and led the charge to integrate TCP/IP into BSD.

The TCP/IP stack provided a standardized way for computers to communicate over networks, which was crucial for the development of the Internet. The BSD implementation was notable for its ease of use and efficiency. It allowed multiple machines to communicate seamlessly, paving the way for the Internet as we know it today.

$$\text{Throughput} = \frac{\text{Data Sent}}{\text{Time Taken}} \tag{15}$$

This equation illustrates the importance of optimizing data transmission rates, a challenge that the BSD team tackled head-on. They implemented various algorithms to enhance throughput and reduce latency, making BSD a preferred choice for network applications.

The Sockets API

To further enhance networking capabilities, BSD introduced the Sockets API, a programming interface that allowed developers to create networked applications easily. This API abstracted the complexities of network communication, enabling developers to focus on building applications rather than getting bogged down by the underlying protocols.

The Sockets API made it possible to establish connections, send and receive data, and handle network errors with relative ease. This innovation was instrumental in popularizing network programming and remains a cornerstone of modern networking in operating systems today.

File System Innovations: The Fast File System (FFS)

While networking was a major focus, Joy and his team also recognized the need for efficient file storage and retrieval. Enter the Fast File System (FFS), which was introduced in BSD 4.2. FFS was designed to address the limitations of traditional Unix file systems, which struggled with performance as disk sizes grew.

FFS introduced several key innovations:

- **Block Allocation:** FFS employed a new block allocation strategy that minimized fragmentation. By grouping related files together on disk, FFS improved access times and overall performance.

- **Cylinder Groups:** The introduction of cylinder groups allowed the file system to manage data more efficiently. By organizing files into groups based on their physical location on the disk, FFS reduced seek times and increased throughput.

- **Improved Metadata Handling:** FFS optimized the way metadata was stored and accessed, allowing for faster file operations. This was particularly important for systems that needed to handle large volumes of files and directories.

The impact of FFS was profound. It not only improved performance for existing applications but also enabled new use cases that required high-speed data access. As a result, BSD became the go-to choice for servers and workstations that demanded reliability and speed.

Case Study: The Success of BSD in Networking and File Systems

To illustrate the impact of these innovations, consider the case of a university research lab that adopted BSD for its computing needs. The lab required a robust networking solution to facilitate collaboration between researchers across different campuses. With BSD's integrated TCP/IP stack and Sockets API, the lab was able to develop a suite of applications that allowed seamless data sharing and communication.

Furthermore, as the lab's data storage needs grew, the efficiency of FFS allowed them to manage large datasets without sacrificing performance. Researchers could access and analyze data faster than ever, leading to breakthroughs in their respective fields.

Conclusion: The Lasting Impact of BSD Innovations

The innovations in networking and file systems introduced by Bill Joy and the BSD team have had a lasting impact on the computing world. The integration of TCP/IP and the development of the Sockets API laid the groundwork for the Internet, while the Fast File System set new standards for file management.

These innovations not only made BSD a fucking powerhouse in the operating system landscape but also influenced countless other systems that followed. The principles established in BSD continue to resonate in modern computing, proving that Joy's vision was not just about creating software; it was about shaping the future of technology itself.

The Future of BSD: Why Joy's Fucking Legacy Still Influences Modern Operating Systems

Bill Joy's contributions to the Berkeley Software Distribution (BSD) operating system have left an indelible mark on the world of computing, and his legacy continues to shape modern operating systems in profound ways. This section delves into the enduring influence of BSD, examining its foundational concepts, the challenges it faces today, and how Joy's vision continues to inspire innovation in the tech landscape.

The Enduring Influence of BSD

BSD was not just another operating system; it was a revolutionary platform that introduced several key concepts that are still relevant in today's computing environments. One of the most significant contributions of BSD is its robust networking capabilities. The implementation of the Transmission Control Protocol/Internet Protocol (TCP/IP) stack in BSD laid the groundwork for the modern Internet. As we analyze the impact of Joy's work, we must recognize that the principles of modularity and interoperability that he championed are now cornerstones of contemporary operating systems.

$$\text{Modularity} = \frac{\text{Functionality}}{\text{Complexity}} \qquad (16)$$

This equation highlights the importance of creating modular components that can function independently while contributing to the overall complexity of the system. Joy's vision of a modular architecture is evident in modern operating systems, where microservices and containerization have become standard practices.

Challenges Facing BSD Today

Despite its historical significance, BSD faces challenges in maintaining relevance in a rapidly evolving technological landscape dominated by Linux and proprietary systems. One of the primary issues is the perception of BSD as less user-friendly compared to its counterparts. While BSD offers robustness and security, it often lacks the extensive user support and community engagement that Linux enjoys. This disparity can be illustrated by the following equation:

$$\text{User Adoption} = \frac{\text{Community Support}}{\text{Learning Curve}} \qquad (17)$$

Here, we see that user adoption is inversely proportional to the learning curve. The more accessible an operating system is, the more likely it is to gain traction among users. Joy's legacy in fostering open-source collaboration is crucial for addressing this challenge. By encouraging a vibrant community around BSD, we can enhance its user-friendliness and promote wider adoption.

Examples of BSD's Modern Influence

The influence of BSD can be observed in several modern operating systems and technologies. For instance, Apple's macOS and iOS are built on a BSD foundation, incorporating many of the system's principles and features. The security model and file system architecture of these operating systems are direct descendants of Joy's innovations.

Moreover, FreeBSD, one of the most prominent BSD variants, continues to be a preferred choice for server environments due to its performance and advanced networking features. Many cloud service providers leverage FreeBSD for its scalability and reliability, demonstrating that Joy's vision of a powerful, open-source operating system remains relevant in today's cloud-centric world.

The Open-Source Philosophy and Future Innovations

Joy's belief in the open-source philosophy is perhaps his most significant legacy. He argued that software should be free and accessible, a notion that has become a rallying cry for developers worldwide. The rise of collaborative platforms like GitHub and the popularity of open-source projects underscore the relevance of this philosophy in driving innovation.

As we look to the future, the principles laid out by Joy are more critical than ever. The ongoing development of projects like OpenBSD and NetBSD exemplifies how the open-source community continues to build on Joy's foundation. These projects not only preserve the spirit of BSD but also innovate in areas such as security and portability.

Conclusion: A Lasting Legacy

In conclusion, Bill Joy's legacy within the BSD operating system is a testament to his visionary thinking and commitment to open-source principles. The influence of BSD is evident in modern operating systems, networking protocols, and the broader tech community. As we navigate the complexities of today's computing environment, Joy's principles of modularity, interoperability, and collaboration will continue to inspire future generations of programmers and technologists. The future of BSD, while facing challenges, remains bright, fueled by the enduring spirit of innovation that Joy instilled in the world of software development.

Bill Joy's Fucking Impact on the Open-Source Community

How Bill Joy Fought the Fucking Corporate Mentality of Closed Software

Bill Joy, a name synonymous with innovation and open-source philosophy, emerged as a fierce advocate against the corporate mentality that sought to enclose software behind impenetrable walls. In an era where proprietary software reigned supreme, Joy's vision for a more open and collaborative approach to computing was nothing short of revolutionary. This section delves into the strategies and philosophies that defined Joy's battle against the suffocating grip of closed software.

The Corporate Landscape of Closed Software

During the late 20th century, the tech industry was dominated by a few powerful corporations that prioritized profit over progress. Companies like Microsoft and IBM thrived on a closed-source model, where software was treated as a trade secret, tightly controlled, and sold to consumers without any means for modification or redistribution. This approach not only stifled innovation but also limited the potential for collaboration among developers.

Joy recognized that this corporate mentality created a barrier to entry for aspiring programmers and hindered the growth of the software ecosystem. The closed nature of proprietary software meant that developers could not learn from one another, nor could they build upon existing technologies to create new solutions. The lack of transparency fostered an environment where bugs and security vulnerabilities could fester, unaddressed by a community that had no access to the source code.

The Birth of BSD: A Counter-Movement

In response to the restrictive nature of proprietary software, Joy spearheaded the development of the Berkeley Software Distribution (BSD) while at the University of California, Berkeley. BSD was not just an operating system; it was a manifesto for open-source principles. Joy and his team took the UNIX operating system, which was originally developed by AT&T, and reimagined it as a freely distributable and modifiable platform.

The decision to create BSD was rooted in the belief that software should be accessible to all. Joy famously stated, "The most important thing is to be able to share your work." This ethos was a direct challenge to the corporate mentality that sought to restrict access and control over software. By releasing BSD into the public domain, Joy empowered a generation of developers to learn, innovate, and contribute to the software landscape.

Legal Battles and Advocacy

Joy's fight against closed software was not without its challenges. One of the most significant battles came against AT&T, which claimed ownership over the UNIX code that BSD was based on. In a landmark case, Joy and his team had to navigate the murky waters of intellectual property law to defend their right to distribute BSD.

This legal struggle highlighted the broader implications of closed software. Joy argued that proprietary control over software not only limited innovation but also created a culture of fear among developers who were wary of legal repercussions for using or modifying existing code. His advocacy for open-source principles extended beyond the confines of BSD; it became a rallying cry for developers around the world.

The Philosophy of Open-Source Software

At the heart of Joy's fight against the corporate mentality was a deeply ingrained philosophy that software should be free. This belief was not merely about the absence of a price tag; it was about the freedom to use, modify, and share software without restriction. Joy's vision was encapsulated in the phrase, "Software is like air; it should be free."

This philosophy laid the groundwork for the open-source movement, which gained momentum in the 1990s and early 2000s. Joy's influence can be seen in the creation of licenses like the GNU General Public License (GPL), which enshrined the principles of free software and ensured that future generations of developers could build upon the work of their predecessors without fear of corporate retribution.

Case Studies: The Impact of Open-Source Software

The impact of Joy's fight against the corporate mentality of closed software can be seen in numerous case studies. One notable example is the rise of the Linux operating system, which was born out of the open-source philosophy that Joy championed. Linus Torvalds, inspired by the principles of BSD, created Linux as a free alternative to proprietary operating systems. Today, Linux powers everything from smartphones to supercomputers, a testament to the power of open collaboration.

Another example is the Apache HTTP Server, which became the most widely used web server software in the world. The success of Apache can be attributed to the open-source model that Joy fought for, allowing developers to contribute to and improve the software collaboratively.

The Future of Open-Source Software

As we look to the future, the legacy of Bill Joy's fight against the corporate mentality of closed software continues to resonate. The open-source movement has grown exponentially, with companies like Red Hat and Canonical thriving on the principles of collaboration and transparency. Joy's vision has not only shaped the way software is developed but has also influenced the culture of the tech industry as a whole.

In conclusion, Bill Joy's relentless battle against the corporate mentality of closed software has left an indelible mark on the world of technology. His advocacy for open-source principles has fostered a culture of innovation, collaboration, and accessibility that continues to inspire developers today. As we navigate the complexities of modern computing, we must remember Joy's mantra: that software should be free, and that the true power of technology lies in our ability to share and collaborate.

The Fucking Philosophical Belief That Programming Knowledge Should Be Shared

Bill Joy, the fucking visionary behind some of the most groundbreaking software innovations, firmly believed in the fundamental principle that programming knowledge should be shared. This belief was not just a personal mantra; it was a guiding philosophy that shaped the very fabric of the open-source movement and influenced countless developers around the globe.

The Roots of Open-Source Philosophy

At the core of Joy's philosophy lies the idea that knowledge is a collective resource. He viewed programming not merely as a technical skill but as a form of art that thrives on collaboration and community. This perspective is deeply rooted in the early days of computing, where programmers often shared their code and ideas freely. Joy's experiences at the University of California, Berkeley, were pivotal in reinforcing this belief.

During his time at Berkeley, Joy and his team developed the Berkeley Software Distribution (BSD), a Unix derivative that was revolutionary for its time. The BSD project was a collaborative effort that brought together brilliant minds, and the ethos of sharing knowledge was evident. Joy understood that the more programmers shared their insights and code, the more robust and innovative the software ecosystem would become. This realization laid the groundwork for the open-source movement.

Case Studies: The Open-Source Movement

The impact of Joy's philosophy can be seen in the development of various open-source projects that have transformed the technology landscape. For instance, the Linux operating system, which emerged as a direct descendant of the BSD systems, embodies the spirit of sharing knowledge. Linus Torvalds, the creator of Linux, was heavily influenced by the collaborative culture that Joy championed.

The success of Linux can be attributed to its open-source nature, allowing thousands of developers to contribute to its codebase. This collaborative model not only accelerated innovation but also democratized access to technology. The fundamental belief that programming knowledge should be shared created a community of developers who were passionate about building something greater than themselves.

The Fucking Importance of Documentation and Education

Joy's commitment to sharing knowledge extended beyond code. He recognized the importance of documentation and education in empowering the next generation of programmers. The BSD project was notable for its comprehensive documentation, which provided users with the tools they needed to understand and modify the software. Joy's belief was that effective documentation was essential for fostering a community of learners and contributors.

Moreover, Joy's involvement in educational initiatives, such as teaching programming at Berkeley, underscored his dedication to sharing knowledge. He understood that by educating others, he was not just imparting skills but also inspiring a new wave of innovation.

Challenges and Resistance

Despite the clear benefits of sharing knowledge, Joy faced significant challenges and resistance from the corporate world. The rise of proprietary software in the 1980s and 1990s created a stark contrast to the open-source philosophy. Companies often viewed software as a product to be sold, rather than a collaborative endeavor. This mentality was epitomized by the likes of Microsoft, which aggressively protected its intellectual property.

Joy was a vocal critic of this corporate mentality, arguing that it stifled innovation and limited access to technology. He believed that when knowledge is hoarded, it creates barriers to entry for aspiring programmers and hinders the growth of the tech industry. Joy's unwavering stance on open-source principles positioned him as a champion for the rights of developers and users alike.

The Legacy of Sharing Knowledge

The legacy of Bill Joy's belief in sharing programming knowledge is evident in the thriving open-source community today. Projects like GitHub have revolutionized the way developers collaborate, allowing for seamless sharing of code and ideas. The open-source movement has not only led to the development of powerful software but has also fostered a culture of inclusivity and collaboration.

Joy's influence can also be seen in the rise of coding bootcamps and online learning platforms that emphasize the importance of community and shared knowledge. These initiatives reflect Joy's vision of a world where programming skills are accessible to all, regardless of background or resources.

Conclusion: The Fucking Future of Knowledge Sharing

As we look to the future, Joy's philosophy of sharing programming knowledge remains as relevant as ever. The tech industry continues to grapple with the balance between proprietary and open-source software, but the momentum towards collaboration and openness is undeniable. Joy's legacy serves as a reminder that the true power of technology lies in its ability to bring people together, and that sharing knowledge is not just a noble ideal, but a fucking necessity for innovation.

In conclusion, Bill Joy's unwavering belief that programming knowledge should be shared has fundamentally shaped the tech landscape. His contributions to open-source software and his commitment to education and collaboration have paved the way for a more inclusive and innovative future. As we continue to navigate the complexities of the digital age, let us honor Joy's legacy by embracing the spirit of sharing and collaboration that he championed throughout his career.

Case Studies: How BSD Laid the Fucking Groundwork for Linux and Modern Operating Systems

The Berkeley Software Distribution (BSD) operating system, developed at the University of California, Berkeley, in the late 1970s and early 1980s, serves as a cornerstone for modern operating systems, including Linux. In this section, we delve into the case studies that illustrate how BSD's innovations and philosophies laid the groundwork for the open-source movement and shaped the development of contemporary systems.

The UNIX Heritage: BSD's Roots

At its core, BSD was derived from AT&T's UNIX, which was a proprietary operating system. Bill Joy and his colleagues at Berkeley sought to enhance UNIX by adding features that would make it more powerful and accessible. This was a time when the tech landscape was dominated by corporate control over software, and Joy's team was determined to break free from that mold. The first version of BSD, released in 1977, introduced several key features:

- **Networking Capabilities:** BSD integrated the Berkeley Sockets API, which allowed different processes to communicate over a network. This was revolutionary, as it laid the foundation for the Internet as we know it today.

- **File System Improvements:** The Fast File System (FFS) was introduced in BSD, significantly enhancing file access speed and efficiency. This innovation influenced future file systems in various operating systems.

- **User-Friendly Enhancements:** BSD introduced a range of user commands and utilities that made the system more accessible to users, promoting the idea that powerful tools should be available to everyone, not just a select few.

These innovations not only improved the functionality of UNIX but also set a precedent for the open-source philosophy that would later define Linux.

Case Study: The Birth of TCP/IP

One of the most significant contributions of BSD to the world of computing was the implementation of the Transmission Control Protocol/Internet Protocol (TCP/IP) stack. In the early 1980s, as the Internet began to take shape, Joy and his team recognized the need for a robust networking protocol. The adoption of TCP/IP in BSD was not just a technical achievement; it was a philosophical one.

$$\text{TCP/IP} = (\text{Transport Layer}) + (\text{Internet Layer}) \qquad (18)$$

This equation represents the two fundamental layers of TCP/IP, which enabled reliable communication across diverse networks. By integrating TCP/IP into BSD,

Joy's team facilitated the development of a global network of interconnected systems. This move was pivotal, as it allowed BSD to become the go-to operating system for academic institutions and research organizations, further spreading its influence.

Case Study: The BSD License

Another critical aspect of BSD's legacy is the BSD License, which was among the first open-source licenses. Unlike the restrictive licenses prevalent at the time, the BSD License allowed users to modify and redistribute the software with minimal restrictions. This was a radical departure from the traditional software distribution model and directly influenced the licensing of Linux and many other open-source projects.

The BSD License can be summarized as follows:

- **Freedom to Use:** Users can run the software for any purpose.

- **Freedom to Modify:** Users can alter the source code to suit their needs.

- **Freedom to Distribute:** Users can share the original or modified software with others.

This framework encouraged collaboration and innovation, laying the groundwork for the open-source movement that Linux would later embody. The BSD License has influenced numerous software projects, establishing a culture of sharing and cooperation in the software development community.

Case Study: The Impact on Linux

Linus Torvalds, the creator of Linux, openly acknowledged the influence of BSD on his work. When Torvalds began developing Linux in 1991, he drew inspiration from the principles and features of BSD. The modular design, networking capabilities, and user-friendly utilities of BSD served as a model for Linux's development.

> "I looked at MINIX, but I was also inspired by BSD. The way it was structured and the features it offered were exactly what I wanted to replicate and build upon."

This acknowledgment highlights the direct lineage from BSD to Linux, showcasing how Joy's innovations provided the necessary foundation for the next generation of operating systems.

Case Study: The Legacy of BSD in Modern Systems

The influence of BSD extends far beyond Linux. Many modern operating systems, including FreeBSD, OpenBSD, and NetBSD, are direct descendants of the original BSD codebase. These systems have continued to innovate, introducing features such as advanced security protocols, improved networking stacks, and cutting-edge file systems.

Moreover, BSD's impact can be seen in commercial operating systems as well. Apple's macOS is built on a BSD foundation, incorporating many of the features and philosophies that Joy and his team pioneered. This cross-pollination of ideas exemplifies how BSD's legacy continues to shape the technological landscape.

Conclusion: The Enduring Influence of BSD

In conclusion, the case studies presented in this section illustrate how BSD laid the fucking groundwork for Linux and modern operating systems. Through its innovative features, open-source licensing, and philosophical approach to software development, BSD not only challenged the status quo but also inspired a generation of developers to embrace the open-source model. Bill Joy's vision and leadership in the creation of BSD have left an indelible mark on the world of computing, ensuring that his legacy will continue to influence technology for decades to come.

How Joy's Fucking Work Inspired an Entire Generation of Open-Source Developers

Bill Joy's influence on the open-source movement is not just significant; it's fucking monumental. His work on the Berkeley Software Distribution (BSD) and the advocacy for open-source principles laid the groundwork for a culture of collaboration and innovation that continues to thrive today. This section explores how Joy's contributions inspired a generation of developers to embrace open-source software, fostering a community where knowledge is shared freely and creativity is unleashed.

The Open-Source Philosophy: A Radical Departure

At the heart of Joy's philosophy was the belief that software should be free. This wasn't just a casual thought; it was a fucking revolutionary stance at a time when proprietary software dominated the landscape. Joy's work on BSD was rooted in the idea that sharing code could lead to better software for everyone. This was a stark contrast to the corporate mentality of the time, where companies hoarded their code like it was fucking gold.

The BSD license, which allowed users to modify and distribute the software freely, became a beacon for developers disillusioned with the restrictive nature of proprietary software. Joy's vision was encapsulated in the phrase: "Good software is a product of many minds." This notion resonated deeply with a generation of developers, sparking a movement that prioritized collaboration over competition.

Case Studies: The Ripple Effect of BSD

The impact of BSD on the open-source community can be illustrated through several key case studies. One of the most notable is the emergence of Linux. Linus Torvalds, inspired by the principles established by Joy and the BSD community, set out to create his own operating system kernel. The result? A fucking revolution in computing. Linux became the cornerstone of open-source operating systems, powering everything from servers to smartphones.

Another example is the development of the Apache HTTP Server. The Apache project was born out of the need for a robust, open-source web server, and it drew heavily from the collaborative spirit that Joy championed. The result was a server that became the backbone of the web, demonstrating how open-source principles could lead to technological advancements that benefited all.

The Educational Impact: Cultivating a New Generation

Joy's influence extended beyond just software; it permeated educational institutions and programming communities. Universities began to adopt open-source software in their curricula, teaching students not only how to code but also the importance of collaboration and sharing knowledge. This shift was pivotal in shaping a generation of developers who understood that the future of technology lay in open-source practices.

The creation of platforms like GitHub further exemplifies this shift. By providing a space for developers to collaborate, share, and contribute to projects, GitHub became a fucking playground for open-source enthusiasts. Joy's legacy is evident in the way these platforms have empowered developers to work together across the globe, breaking down geographical barriers and fostering a sense of community.

The Role of Community and Mentorship

Joy didn't just inspire through his work; he actively engaged with the developer community. His willingness to share knowledge and mentor aspiring programmers created a ripple effect that encouraged others to do the same. The open-source community thrives on mentorship, and Joy's example set a fucking standard for what it means to be a leader in this space.

Projects like FreeBSD and OpenBSD not only benefited from Joy's initial contributions but also from the culture of mentorship that he fostered. Developers were encouraged to contribute, learn, and grow, creating a self-sustaining ecosystem where innovation could flourish. This culture is a direct result of Joy's belief that knowledge should be shared, not hoarded.

Challenges and Resilience in the Open-Source Community

Despite the enthusiasm surrounding open-source software, challenges remained. The corporate world often viewed open-source as a threat, leading to legal battles and attempts to undermine the movement. However, Joy's work provided a fucking blueprint for resilience. The principles he championed helped the open-source community navigate these challenges, reinforcing the idea that collaboration could triumph over corporate greed.

For instance, the legal battles surrounding the GNU General Public License (GPL) were influenced by the groundwork laid by Joy and the BSD community. The GPL's emphasis on copyleft and ensuring that software remained free for all users echoed Joy's vision and provided a framework for developers to protect their contributions.

The Ongoing Legacy of Bill Joy's Work

Today, the open-source movement continues to thrive, and its roots can be traced back to the principles that Bill Joy espoused. The tools and technologies that emerged from this movement have transformed the tech landscape, from cloud computing to artificial intelligence. Joy's vision of a world where software is free and accessible has inspired countless developers to push the boundaries of what's possible.

As we look to the future, Joy's legacy serves as a reminder of the power of collaboration and the importance of keeping software open. The fucking spirit of innovation that he ignited in the open-source community is alive and well, driving the next generation of developers to create, share, and revolutionize the tech world.

In conclusion, Bill Joy's work did not just inspire a generation of open-source developers; it created a fucking movement that changed the course of technology. His relentless pursuit of innovation and belief in the power of collaboration have left an indelible mark on the tech industry, ensuring that his legacy will continue to influence generations to come.

The Future of Open-Source Software: Will Bill Joy's Fucking Vision Continue to Drive Innovation?

Bill Joy's legacy in the world of open-source software is not merely a chapter in the annals of computing history; it is a living, breathing testament to the power of collaboration, innovation, and the belief that software should be free for all. As we gaze into the future of open-source software, we must ask ourselves: Will Joy's fucking vision continue to drive innovation, or will it be stifled by the encroaching shadows of corporate interests and proprietary software?

The landscape of open-source software has evolved dramatically since Joy first championed the cause. With the rise of cloud computing, containerization, and microservices, the principles of open-source have found new relevance. Companies like Red Hat and Canonical have demonstrated that open-source models can thrive commercially while remaining true to the foundational ideals of transparency and collaboration. This duality is essential; it allows for the sustainability of open-source projects while ensuring that they remain accessible to developers worldwide.

One of the most pressing challenges facing the open-source community today is the issue of sustainability. Many projects rely heavily on volunteer contributions, which can lead to burnout and inconsistency. As Joy once noted, "Innovation is not just about technology; it's about people." The future of open-source will depend on finding ways to support and incentivize contributors. This could involve creating more formalized funding models, such as crowdfunding or sponsorships, to ensure that projects can maintain momentum and attract new talent.

$$\text{Sustainability} = \text{Funding} + \text{Community Engagement} + \text{Project Management} \tag{19}$$

The equation above illustrates the multifaceted approach needed to sustain open-source projects. It is not enough to simply have funding; community engagement and effective project management are equally critical. Joy's philosophy emphasized the importance of community, and this remains true today. Projects like the Linux kernel and Apache HTTP Server have thrived not only because of their technical merits but also due to the robust communities that support them.

Furthermore, the rise of artificial intelligence (AI) and machine learning (ML) presents both opportunities and challenges for open-source software. On one hand, open-source frameworks like TensorFlow and PyTorch have democratized access to powerful AI tools, enabling developers to innovate without the constraints of proprietary software. On the other hand, as AI becomes increasingly integrated into software development, the potential for proprietary solutions to dominate the market grows. Joy's vision of an open-source future must adapt to ensure that these new technologies remain accessible and that the community can continue to contribute to their evolution.

$$\text{Innovation Rate} = \frac{\text{Open-Source Contributions}}{\text{Proprietary Solutions}} \qquad (20)$$

This equation highlights the need for a balanced ecosystem where open-source contributions can compete with proprietary solutions. The future of open-source innovation hinges on the ability of the community to leverage new technologies while remaining vigilant against the pitfalls of commercialization.

Moreover, the global nature of software development today means that open-source projects can benefit from a diverse range of perspectives and expertise. As Joy famously stated, "The great thing about open-source is that it's not just about the code; it's about the people." This sentiment rings true as we witness the rise of international collaborations on platforms like GitHub and GitLab. These platforms have made it easier than ever for developers from different backgrounds to come together, share ideas, and contribute to projects that can have a global impact.

However, with this increased collaboration comes the challenge of maintaining quality and coherence within projects. As more contributors join, ensuring that the code remains clean, efficient, and well-documented becomes paramount. This is where Joy's emphasis on mentorship and guidance comes into play. Experienced developers must take on the role of mentors, helping to onboard newcomers and instilling best practices that will uphold the integrity of open-source software.

$$\text{Code Quality} = \text{Mentorship} + \text{Documentation} + \text{Review Process} \qquad (21)$$

This equation suggests that high-quality code in open-source projects is a product of effective mentorship, thorough documentation, and a robust review process. Joy's legacy as a mentor to countless developers underscores the importance of these elements in fostering a healthy open-source ecosystem.

As we look to the future, it is clear that Bill Joy's fucking vision for open-source software is more relevant than ever. The principles he championed—collaboration, transparency, and community engagement—are the bedrock upon which the future of technology will be built. However, the challenges are real, and the path forward requires a concerted effort from all stakeholders involved in open-source development.

In conclusion, the future of open-source software is bright, but it will require vigilance, innovation, and a commitment to the ideals that Bill Joy so passionately advocated. As developers, we must strive to honor his legacy by fostering an environment where creativity can flourish, knowledge can be shared freely, and innovation can continue to thrive. If we can navigate the complexities of modern technology while remaining true to the spirit of open-source, then Joy's vision will undoubtedly continue to drive innovation for generations to come.

Sun Microsystems and the Creation of Java

From Berkeley to Sun: How Bill Joy Made His Fucking Mark on Silicon Valley

The Founding of Sun Microsystems: How Joy Helped Build One of the Fucking Most Influential Tech Companies of the 80s

In the early 1980s, the tech landscape was ripe for disruption, and at the forefront of this revolution was Bill Joy. After his groundbreaking work on the Berkeley Software Distribution (BSD), Joy was ready to take on a new challenge. This challenge manifested in the form of Sun Microsystems, a company that would go on to become one of the most influential tech giants of the decade. Founded in 1982 by four Stanford University alumni, including Joy, Sun Microsystems was born out of a vision to create powerful workstations that leveraged the capabilities of UNIX.

The Vision Behind Sun

The original idea behind Sun was straightforward yet revolutionary: to create a workstation that was not only powerful but also accessible to a wider audience. Joy, with his deep understanding of UNIX and networking, recognized that the future of computing lay in making powerful computing resources available to everyone, not just the elite few. He famously articulated this vision with the phrase, "The network is the computer," which became a guiding principle for the company.

The company's name, SUN, originally stood for Stanford University Network, underscored the academic roots of its founders. Joy, alongside his co-founders, aimed to leverage their academic experience to create a company that would push the boundaries of what was possible in computing.

Building the First Workstations

One of the first products developed by Sun Microsystems was the Sun-1 workstation, which was based on the Motorola 68000 microprocessor. This workstation was revolutionary for its time, offering features that were previously only available on much more expensive machines. The Sun-1 was equipped with a graphical user interface and networking capabilities, allowing users to connect to other systems seamlessly.

The architecture of the Sun-1 was a significant departure from traditional computing models, which often relied on mainframes. Instead, Joy and his team focused on creating a distributed computing environment where multiple workstations could communicate and share resources. This approach not only improved efficiency but also laid the groundwork for the networked computing paradigm that would dominate the industry in the years to come.

Challenges and Breakthroughs

However, the journey was not without its challenges. One of the significant hurdles Sun faced was competition from established players in the market, such as IBM and DEC, who had a stronghold on the workstation and server markets. To differentiate itself, Sun had to innovate continuously.

Joy's experience with BSD played a crucial role in this innovation. The open-source nature of BSD allowed Sun to build on existing technologies without the constraints of proprietary systems. This adaptability enabled Sun to develop a robust operating system, known as SunOS, which was based on UNIX. The combination of powerful hardware and a flexible operating system set Sun apart from its competitors.

$$\text{Performance} = f(\text{CPU Speed, Memory, I/O Operations}) \qquad (22)$$

In this equation, performance is a function of the CPU speed, memory capacity, and input/output operations, all of which were significantly enhanced in Sun's workstations compared to existing models. Joy's relentless pursuit of performance optimization led to innovations in hardware design and software efficiency.

FROM BERKELEY TO SUN: HOW BILL JOY MADE HIS FUCKING MARK ON SILICON VALLEY

The Culture of Innovation

Joy's leadership style fostered a culture of innovation within Sun. He encouraged his team to experiment, take risks, and challenge the status quo. This environment attracted some of the brightest minds in technology, creating a feedback loop of creativity and excellence.

One notable example of this culture was the development of the Network File System (NFS), which allowed different machines to share files over a network seamlessly. This innovation was a direct result of Joy's belief in the power of networking and collaboration, and it became a cornerstone of modern computing.

The Impact of Sun Microsystems

By the late 1980s, Sun Microsystems had established itself as a powerhouse in the tech industry. The company's workstations were in high demand, and its influence extended beyond hardware into software and networking. Joy's vision had not only built a successful company but had also changed the landscape of computing.

The success of Sun Microsystems can be attributed to Joy's innovative thinking, technical expertise, and unwavering commitment to making computing accessible. The company paved the way for future developments in distributed computing, setting the stage for the internet revolution that would follow.

In conclusion, the founding of Sun Microsystems was a pivotal moment in the history of technology. Bill Joy's contributions were instrumental in shaping the company's trajectory and establishing it as one of the most influential tech companies of the 1980s. His legacy continues to resonate in the modern tech landscape, where the principles of open-source software and networking remain integral to innovation.

How Bill Joy's Fucking Vision and Technical Prowess Shaped Sun's Fucking Direction

Bill Joy, the fucking mastermind behind some of the most transformative technologies of the late 20th century, didn't just stumble into Sun Microsystems; he stormed in with a vision that would redefine the landscape of computing. When Joy co-founded Sun in 1982, he brought not only his technical prowess but also a unique perspective on what computing could and should be. His insights were instrumental in steering the company towards a trajectory that would see it become a titan in the tech industry.

The Vision for Networked Computing

At the heart of Joy's vision was the belief that computing should be inherently networked. In an era when personal computers were becoming commonplace but largely isolated, Joy foresaw a world where machines communicated seamlessly over networks. This foresight led to the development of the Network File System (NFS), a protocol that allowed different machines to share files as if they were on the same local disk.

$$\text{NFS}(x) = \text{Local Access}(x) \oplus \text{Remote Access}(x) \qquad (23)$$

Where x represents a file or resource, and $\oplus$ denotes the seamless integration of local and remote access. This innovation not only enhanced productivity but also laid the groundwork for the modern internet, where sharing and collaboration are fundamental.

The Technical Prowess Behind SPARC

Joy's technical expertise was also pivotal in the development of the SPARC (Scalable Processor Architecture) microprocessor. Recognizing the limitations of existing architectures, Joy championed a design that prioritized scalability and performance. The SPARC architecture was based on the Reduced Instruction Set Computing (RISC) principles, which emphasized a small, highly optimized instruction set to improve execution speed.

$$\text{Performance} \propto \frac{\text{Instructions Executed}}{\text{Cycles Per Instruction} \times \text{Clock Cycle Time}} \qquad (24)$$

This equation illustrates the performance gains achieved through RISC, where a reduced number of cycles per instruction leads to faster processing times. Joy's commitment to RISC principles not only propelled Sun's hardware to the forefront of the industry but also influenced countless other architectures that followed.

Fostering a Culture of Innovation

Joy's vision extended beyond technology; he understood that fostering a culture of innovation was crucial for Sun's success. He encouraged open communication and collaboration among engineers, creating an environment where ideas could flourish. This cultural shift was encapsulated in the mantra, "The network is the computer," which emphasized the importance of connectivity and collaboration.

$$\text{Innovation} = \text{Collaboration} + \text{Creativity} \qquad (25)$$

Joy believed that innovation was the product of collaboration and creativity, and he actively sought to break down silos within the organization. By promoting interdisciplinary teamwork, he ensured that diverse perspectives contributed to the development of groundbreaking technologies.

Facing Challenges Head-On

Of course, Joy's journey was not without its challenges. As Sun grew, so did the complexity of managing a rapidly expanding organization. Joy faced the daunting task of balancing the need for innovation with the realities of business operations. His solution was to instill a sense of purpose among employees, aligning their individual goals with the company's mission.

$$\text{Alignment} = \text{Individual Goals} \cap \text{Company Mission} \qquad (26)$$

Where $\cap$ denotes the intersection of individual aspirations and collective objectives. This alignment helped to mitigate conflicts and fostered a shared commitment to Sun's vision.

Legacy of Joy's Vision at Sun

The impact of Bill Joy's vision and technical prowess at Sun Microsystems is immeasurable. Under his guidance, Sun became synonymous with innovation in the tech industry. The company's commitment to open standards and interoperability can be traced back to Joy's belief that technology should empower users rather than restrict them.

As we reflect on Joy's legacy, it is clear that his vision was not merely about creating products; it was about shaping the future of computing itself. His contributions laid the foundation for many of the technologies we take for granted today, from networked computing to the principles of open-source software.

In conclusion, Bill Joy's fucking vision and technical prowess not only shaped the direction of Sun Microsystems but also left an indelible mark on the entire tech industry. His relentless pursuit of innovation, combined with a deep understanding of the potential of computing, transformed Sun into a powerhouse and paved the way for the interconnected world we inhabit today.

Case Studies: The Fucking Key Projects Joy Worked On During His Time at Sun

During his tenure at Sun Microsystems, Bill Joy was instrumental in a variety of groundbreaking projects that not only shaped the company but also had a lasting impact on the technology landscape. This section delves into some of the most significant projects Joy contributed to, showcasing his innovative spirit and technical prowess.

1. The Development of Solaris

One of the most pivotal projects Joy worked on at Sun was the development of the Solaris operating system. Solaris was built on the foundation of SunOS and represented a significant evolution in Unix-based operating systems.

Theoretical Framework Solaris introduced several key features that enhanced its performance and usability:

- **Scalability:** Solaris was designed to scale efficiently across multiple processors, making it suitable for enterprise-level applications.
- **Networking:** Joy's team integrated advanced networking capabilities, including support for TCP/IP and NFS (Network File System), which facilitated file sharing across networks.
- **Security:** The implementation of role-based access control (RBAC) was a direct response to the growing need for secure computing environments.

Challenges and Solutions The development of Solaris was not without its challenges. One significant problem was ensuring compatibility with existing Unix applications while introducing new features. Joy and his team tackled this by adopting a modular architecture, allowing for backward compatibility while enabling the addition of new functionalities.

Impact Solaris quickly became a preferred choice for businesses due to its robust performance and reliability, cementing Sun's reputation in the enterprise market.

2. Network File System (NFS)

Another landmark project was the creation of the Network File System (NFS), which revolutionized how files were accessed over a network.

Theoretical Framework   NFS allowed users to access files on remote systems as if they were local, breaking down geographical barriers in data access. The architecture of NFS is based on the client-server model, where:

$$\text{NFS Client} \leftrightarrow \text{NFS Server} \qquad (27)$$

Problems Addressed   Before NFS, accessing files across different systems required cumbersome methods, often involving physical media. Joy recognized the need for a seamless solution, leading to the development of NFS, which addressed:

- **File Sharing:** Simplified the process of sharing files across different machines.
- **Transparency:** Users could interact with remote files without needing to understand the underlying network complexities.

Example   For instance, a user on a Sun workstation could easily access files stored on a different server by simply referencing the file path as if it were local, such as:

```
/mnt/server/file.txt
```

Legacy   NFS laid the groundwork for modern distributed file systems and remains widely used today, illustrating the far-reaching impact of Joy's vision.

3. The Java Programming Language

Arguably the most significant project Joy was involved in at Sun was the creation of the Java programming language.

Theoretical Framework   Java was designed to be a platform-independent language, which was revolutionary at the time. The mantra "Write Once, Run Anywhere" (WORA) encapsulated this vision. The architecture of Java is built on the following principles:

- **Bytecode:** Java programs are compiled into bytecode, which can be executed on any machine with a Java Virtual Machine (JVM).
- **Garbage Collection:** Automatic memory management was introduced to simplify programming and reduce memory leaks.

Challenges Encountered Developing a language that could run on various platforms posed significant challenges in terms of performance and security. Joy and his team focused on creating a secure execution environment that isolated applications from the underlying system, addressing potential vulnerabilities.

Example An example of Java's platform independence can be illustrated with the following code snippet:

```
public class HelloWorld {
    public static void main(String[] args) {
        System.out.println("Hello, World!");
    }
}
```

This simple program can run on any device with a JVM, demonstrating Java's versatility.

Impact on the Industry Java's introduction marked a pivotal moment in software development, leading to its widespread adoption in web and enterprise applications. Joy's foresight in creating a language that could transcend hardware limitations set the stage for the modern software development landscape.

4. The SPARC Architecture

Joy also played a crucial role in the development of the SPARC (Scalable Processor Architecture) microprocessor architecture, which was designed to support high-performance computing.

Theoretical Framework SPARC was based on the RISC (Reduced Instruction Set Computing) principles, which emphasize a small set of simple instructions that can execute at high speed. The architecture provided:

- **Simplicity:** Fewer instructions allowed for faster execution and easier optimization.

- **Scalability:** Designed to scale from small embedded systems to large servers.

Challenges and Innovations The challenge was to create a processor that could efficiently handle the demands of modern computing while remaining cost-effective. Joy's team innovated by implementing features such as:

- **Register Windows:** This feature allowed for faster context switching, improving performance for multi-threaded applications.
- **Pipeline Architecture:** Enabled multiple instruction stages to be processed simultaneously, enhancing throughput.

Legacy SPARC processors became a staple in high-performance computing environments, further establishing Sun Microsystems as a leader in the technology industry.

5. Collaboration with the Open-Source Community

Throughout his career at Sun, Joy recognized the importance of collaboration with the open-source community. He advocated for open standards and contributed to various projects that emphasized the sharing of knowledge and resources.

Theoretical Framework The philosophy of open-source software is built on the principles of transparency, collaboration, and community-driven development. Joy believed that:

$$\text{Innovation} = \text{Collaboration} + \text{Transparency} \qquad (28)$$

Case Studies Joy's involvement in projects like OpenSolaris and his support for the BSD community exemplified his commitment to open-source principles. These initiatives not only fostered innovation but also cultivated a vibrant ecosystem of developers and users.

Impact The collaboration with the open-source community has had a lasting impact on software development practices, encouraging a culture of sharing and collective problem-solving that persists today.

In summary, Bill Joy's contributions at Sun Microsystems were not just about technological advancements; they were about shaping the future of computing. His projects laid the groundwork for many of the systems and practices that define the tech industry today, showcasing his enduring legacy as a visionary leader in technology.

The Fucking Leadership Challenges at Sun: How Joy Managed the Fucking Tensions Between Innovation and Business

Bill Joy, the fucking visionary behind some of the most revolutionary technologies, faced a unique set of leadership challenges during his tenure at Sun Microsystems. The company was at the forefront of the tech revolution in the 1980s and 1990s, striving to balance the relentless pursuit of innovation with the harsh realities of business. This section explores how Joy navigated these tensions, ensuring that Sun remained a powerhouse of technological advancement while also achieving commercial success.

The Dual Nature of Innovation and Business

At Sun, Joy understood that innovation and business could often be at odds. The drive to create groundbreaking technology often clashed with the need to generate revenue and satisfy stakeholders. This duality can be expressed in the following equation:

$$\text{Innovation} + \text{Business} = \text{Sustainable Growth} \tag{29}$$

Where: - Innovation represents the development of new technologies and products. - Business encompasses the operational and financial strategies necessary for profitability. - Sustainable Growth is the desired outcome that balances both elements.

Joy's approach to this equation was rooted in his belief that innovation should not only be about creating cutting-edge technology but also about delivering value to customers and shareholders. He often emphasized that for innovation to thrive, it needed to be aligned with business objectives.

Fostering a Culture of Innovation

One of Joy's key strategies was to foster a culture of innovation within Sun Microsystems. He encouraged his teams to take risks and experiment with new ideas. Joy believed that a supportive environment was crucial for creativity. He famously stated, "Innovation is not about being right; it's about being willing to fail." This mantra led to the establishment of various internal initiatives aimed at encouraging employees to pursue their ideas without the fear of failure.

For example, Joy implemented "innovation labs" where engineers could work on pet projects that were outside their regular job descriptions. This initiative not only stimulated creativity but also led to the development of products that would later become integral to Sun's success, such as the Solaris operating system.

Balancing Short-Term and Long-Term Goals

Another challenge Joy faced was balancing short-term business pressures with long-term innovation goals. The tech industry is notorious for its rapid pace, and companies often feel compelled to deliver immediate results. Joy recognized that this could stifle true innovation, which often requires time and experimentation.

To address this, Joy employed a strategic framework that allowed Sun to pursue long-term projects while still meeting immediate business needs. He advocated for a portfolio approach, where resources were allocated to both short-term and long-term initiatives. This meant that while some teams focused on developing products for immediate release, others could explore groundbreaking technologies that might not yield results for years.

Navigating Corporate Politics

Navigating the corporate landscape was another significant challenge for Joy. As Sun grew, so did the complexities of its organizational structure. Different departments often had conflicting priorities—sales teams wanted quick-to-market products, while engineering teams aimed for perfection and innovation.

Joy tackled this issue by fostering open communication and collaboration between departments. He implemented regular cross-functional meetings where teams could share their challenges and successes. This transparency not only helped to align goals but also built a sense of camaraderie among employees. Joy's leadership style emphasized the importance of collective success over individual achievements, which helped to mitigate internal conflicts.

Case Studies of Leadership in Action

To illustrate Joy's leadership in managing these tensions, consider the development of the Java programming language. When Sun began the project, there was skepticism about its potential. The sales team was focused on existing products that generated revenue, while the engineering team was excited about the possibilities of Java.

Joy facilitated discussions between both teams, highlighting how Java could open new markets and create opportunities for Sun. He emphasized that investing in Java was not just a gamble but a strategic move that could redefine the company's future.

This collaborative approach helped to secure buy-in from all stakeholders, ultimately leading to Java's successful launch and its profound impact on the internet.

Conclusion: The Legacy of Joy's Leadership

Bill Joy's ability to manage the tensions between innovation and business at Sun Microsystems is a testament to his visionary leadership. By fostering a culture of innovation, balancing short-term and long-term goals, and navigating corporate politics, Joy not only propelled Sun to the forefront of the tech industry but also set a precedent for future leaders. His legacy continues to influence how companies approach the delicate balance between creativity and commercial success in the ever-evolving landscape of technology.

The Future of Sun's Fucking Legacy: Why Joy's Work Continues to Influence Modern Fucking Tech Companies

In the ever-evolving landscape of technology, the legacy of Bill Joy and Sun Microsystems remains a cornerstone of innovation and inspiration. Joy's contributions to the tech world, particularly through his work at Sun, have set a precedent that continues to resonate across modern tech companies. Understanding why Joy's work remains influential involves examining several key factors: the architectural philosophy of software design, the principles of open-source development, and the cultural impact of Joy's leadership style.

Architectural Philosophy

At the heart of Sun Microsystems' approach was the belief in creating systems that could scale and adapt to the changing needs of users. Joy's emphasis on modularity and interoperability can be seen in the design principles of modern software architectures such as microservices. The microservices architecture, which allows for the development of small, independently deployable services, echoes Joy's vision of creating systems that are flexible and capable of evolving over time.

$$\text{Modularity} = \sum_{i=1}^{n} \text{Component}_i \qquad (30)$$

This equation represents the idea that a complex system can be understood as a sum of its parts, each of which can be developed and maintained independently. This principle is evident in platforms like Docker and Kubernetes, which facilitate the deployment and management of microservices, showcasing the long-lasting influence of Joy's architectural philosophy.

Open-Source Principles

Joy was a staunch advocate for open-source software, believing that knowledge should be freely shared. This philosophy is foundational to many modern tech companies, especially in the realm of software development. The rise of collaborative platforms like GitHub is a testament to this legacy. GitHub has transformed how developers collaborate, allowing them to contribute to projects and share their code with the world.

The impact of Joy's open-source advocacy can also be seen in the success of operating systems like Linux, which owe much of their design and community-driven development to the principles Joy championed. The open-source movement has led to a culture of transparency and collaboration, where innovation is driven by community contributions rather than corporate gatekeeping.

Cultural Impact of Leadership

Bill Joy's leadership style emphasized creativity, innovation, and a willingness to take risks. His ability to inspire teams to push the boundaries of what was possible has left a lasting mark on tech culture. Modern tech companies, from startups to established giants, often adopt similar leadership principles, fostering environments that encourage experimentation and bold thinking.

For instance, companies like Google and Netflix have embraced a culture of innovation that mirrors Joy's approach at Sun. Google's famous "20% time" policy, which allows employees to spend a portion of their workweek on personal projects, reflects Joy's belief in empowering individuals to pursue their creative passions. This cultural shift towards valuing innovation and creativity is a direct descendant of Joy's legacy.

Case Studies of Influence

Several contemporary technologies and companies exemplify the lasting influence of Bill Joy's work. For example, the Java programming language, which Joy helped develop, remains one of the most widely used languages in the world. Its principle of "write once, run anywhere" has paved the way for cross-platform development, influencing languages like Kotlin and Swift, which continue to emphasize portability and ease of use.

Moreover, Sun's commitment to network computing laid the groundwork for the cloud computing revolution. Modern cloud platforms, such as Amazon Web Services (AWS) and Microsoft Azure, build upon the networking principles established by Joy and his team at Sun. The shift towards cloud-native applications and services can be traced back to the foundational work done at Sun Microsystems.

Conclusion

Bill Joy's legacy is not merely a historical footnote; it is a living, breathing influence that continues to shape the future of technology. His architectural philosophies, commitment to open-source principles, and innovative leadership style have inspired a generation of developers and tech leaders. As modern tech companies navigate the complexities of a rapidly changing digital landscape, they carry forward the torch lit by Joy and Sun Microsystems, ensuring that the spirit of innovation and collaboration remains at the forefront of technological advancement.

In the words of Joy himself, "Innovation is not about saying yes to everything. It's about saying NO to all but the most crucial features." This mantra continues to guide tech companies as they strive to create meaningful and impactful products in an ever-competitive market. The future of technology is bright, and it is illuminated by the legacy of Bill Joy—a legacy that will undoubtedly influence the tech world for decades to come.

The Fucking Birth of Java: Changing the Internet Forever

How Bill Joy Helped Drive the Fucking Development of Java: A New Language for a New Fucking Era

In the mid-1990s, as the internet began to unfurl its vast potential, the tech world was in dire need of a programming language that could transcend the limitations of its predecessors. Enter Bill Joy, a luminary whose fingerprints were already all over the tech landscape, from the Berkeley Software Distribution (BSD) to the very ethos of open-source software. Joy's involvement in the development of Java was not merely a footnote in his illustrious career; it was a pivotal chapter that would redefine how software interacted with the burgeoning internet.

Java was born out of a need for platform independence. At the time, developers were shackled to the constraints of specific operating systems. The mantra of "write

THE FUCKING BIRTH OF JAVA: CHANGING THE INTERNET FOREVER 55

once, run anywhere" (WORA) became the rallying cry for the Java team, spearheaded by James Gosling at Sun Microsystems, where Joy was a key figure. Joy's vision was clear: a programming language that could operate seamlessly across different platforms, allowing developers to focus on writing code without worrying about the underlying architecture.

The challenge was substantial. Existing languages like C and C++ were powerful but cumbersome when it came to portability. Joy understood that the solution lay in creating a language that was not only syntactically robust but also inherently designed for the networked age. This meant rethinking fundamental programming concepts. Joy and his team opted for a garbage-collected environment, which managed memory automatically, reducing the risk of memory leaks and segmentation faults that often plagued C and C++ developers.

$$\text{Memory Management} = \text{Automatic Garbage Collection} \quad (31)$$

This decision was revolutionary. It allowed developers to focus on building applications rather than wrestling with memory management, a common pitfall that often led to software vulnerabilities. Joy's insistence on safety and reliability became a cornerstone of Java's design philosophy.

Additionally, Joy recognized the importance of security in a networked environment. As the internet opened up, so did the potential for malicious attacks. Java introduced a security model that included a robust set of APIs and a security manager, which allowed developers to specify access controls. This was crucial for running untrusted code, a feature that would become increasingly important as applets and web applications gained traction.

$$\text{Security Model} = \text{APIs} + \text{Security Manager} \quad (32)$$

Joy's foresight in prioritizing security helped establish Java as a trusted language for web applications, a reputation that has persisted to this day. The introduction of the Java Virtual Machine (JVM) was another masterstroke. By abstracting the hardware layer, the JVM allowed Java applications to run on any device that had a JVM installed, thereby fulfilling the WORA promise.

To illustrate the impact of the JVM, consider the following case study: when the first major web browser, Netscape Navigator, integrated Java applets, it opened the floodgates for interactive web applications. Suddenly, developers could create rich user experiences without being tied to a specific platform, a direct result of Joy's vision for a versatile programming language.

The challenges Joy faced during the development of Java were not trivial. There was skepticism in the industry regarding whether a new language could truly compete with established giants. Joy tackled this head-on by fostering a community around Java. He understood that for a language to thrive, it needed a robust ecosystem of developers, libraries, and frameworks. Joy advocated for open-source principles, encouraging collaboration and sharing among developers, which ultimately led to a vibrant Java community.

Furthermore, Joy's leadership at Sun Microsystems was instrumental in navigating the corporate landscape. He championed the idea that Java should be freely available, which aligned with his long-standing belief in the open-source philosophy. This decision not only democratized access to Java but also spurred innovation, as developers worldwide began to contribute to its growth.

In conclusion, Bill Joy's contributions to the development of Java were nothing short of transformative. His foresight in creating a platform-independent, secure, and user-friendly programming language laid the groundwork for the modern internet as we know it. Java's ability to adapt and evolve has allowed it to remain relevant for decades, a testament to Joy's visionary thinking. As we look to the future, it's clear that the legacy of Java and the principles championed by Bill Joy will continue to influence the trajectory of software development and the broader tech landscape.

$$\text{Java Legacy} = \text{Platform Independence} + \text{Security} + \text{Community} \qquad (33)$$

The Fucking Vision Behind Java: Why Joy Believed in a Language that Could Fucking Run Anywhere

When Bill Joy embarked on the journey of creating Java, he envisioned a programming language that transcended the limitations of the existing systems. In a world where software was often tied to specific hardware, Joy sought to develop a language that could operate seamlessly across diverse platforms. This vision was not just about convenience; it was about revolutionizing the way software interacted with hardware, making it more accessible and adaptable for developers and users alike.

The Need for Platform Independence

In the early 1990s, software development was plagued by the notorious phrase, *"Write once, run anywhere"* (WORA). This was a dream that many developers aspired to achieve but rarely succeeded in realizing. The traditional approach required developers to write specific code for each platform, resulting in increased

THE FUCKING BIRTH OF JAVA: CHANGING THE INTERNET FOREVER

development time and costs. Joy recognized that the future of programming lay in a language that could break these chains.

The core of this vision was encapsulated in the concept of **platform independence**. By allowing developers to write code that could be executed on any device with a Java Virtual Machine (JVM), Joy aimed to eliminate the headaches associated with compatibility issues. This approach would not only streamline the development process but also empower developers to focus on innovation rather than being bogged down by the intricacies of hardware differences.

The Role of the Java Virtual Machine

At the heart of Java's platform independence is the Java Virtual Machine (JVM). The JVM acts as an intermediary between the compiled Java code and the underlying hardware. When a developer writes a Java program, it is compiled into an intermediate form known as *bytecode*. This bytecode is not specific to any hardware architecture; instead, it is designed to be executed by the JVM, which can run on any operating system that supports it.

The equation representing this relationship can be simplified as follows:

$$\text{Java Code} \xrightarrow{\text{Compile}} \text{Bytecode} \xrightarrow{\text{Run on JVM}} \text{Platform} \tag{34}$$

This abstraction layer allowed developers to create applications that could function across various environments, from desktop computers to embedded systems, without the need for extensive modifications.

Addressing the Challenges of Portability

While the vision of a universally applicable programming language was enticing, it was not without its challenges. One of the primary issues was ensuring that the Java runtime environment could efficiently execute bytecode on different platforms. Joy and his team had to address concerns related to performance, security, and resource management.

Performance: One of the criticisms of interpreted languages is their performance compared to compiled languages. Joy's team implemented Just-In-Time (JIT) compilation, a technique that compiles bytecode into native machine code at runtime, effectively bridging the gap between interpretation and compilation. This innovation allowed Java applications to run with performance levels comparable to native applications.

Security: As Java gained traction, concerns about security emerged, particularly in the context of running untrusted code over networks. Joy's vision included a robust security model that would allow for safe execution of code. The JVM enforces strict access controls and sandboxing techniques, ensuring that potentially harmful code cannot compromise the host system.

Resource Management: With the diversity of devices that could run Java applications, Joy's team needed to ensure that resource management was efficient. This led to the introduction of automatic garbage collection, a feature that helps manage memory usage without requiring explicit deallocation from developers, thus reducing the risk of memory leaks and improving application stability.

Real-World Examples of Java's Impact

The impact of Joy's vision for Java is evident across various industries. For instance, enterprise applications, such as those used in banking and finance, rely heavily on Java's stability and scalability. Companies like Goldman Sachs and Bank of America have built their trading systems on Java, leveraging its ability to handle massive amounts of data while ensuring security and reliability.

In the realm of mobile computing, Java's influence is undeniable. The Android operating system, which powers billions of devices worldwide, is primarily built on Java. This demonstrates how Joy's vision has not only endured but has also become foundational in shaping the modern technological landscape.

Conclusion: The Enduring Legacy of Joy's Vision

Bill Joy's vision of a language that could truly *"run anywhere"* has fundamentally transformed the software development landscape. By prioritizing platform independence, performance, and security, he laid the groundwork for a programming paradigm that encourages innovation and accessibility. As we continue to navigate the complexities of modern computing, Joy's contributions serve as a reminder of the power of visionary thinking in shaping the future of technology.

In summary, the journey of Java from a mere concept to a ubiquitous force in the tech industry exemplifies the impact of Bill Joy's foresight. The language not only fulfilled its promise of portability but also fostered a community of developers who continue to push the boundaries of what is possible in software development. Joy's legacy is a testament to the fact that when you dare to dream big, the results can be nothing short of extraordinary.

Case Studies: How Java Revolutionized Fucking Web and Enterprise Application Development

Java emerged as a game-changer in the realm of web and enterprise application development, fundamentally altering how developers approached software solutions. This section delves into the transformative impact of Java, exploring key case studies that exemplify its revolutionary role in shaping modern application architecture and deployment.

1. The Rise of Java Applets in Web Development

In the mid-1990s, the internet was evolving rapidly, and developers were seeking ways to create interactive web experiences. Enter Java applets—small applications that could be embedded in web pages. These applets allowed for dynamic content without the need for extensive server-side processing.

$$\text{Applet Execution Time} = \text{Network Latency} + \text{Client Processing Time} \quad (35)$$

The ability to run applets on the client side reduced server load and improved user experience. A notable example is the use of applets in online banking, where institutions like **Bank of America** utilized Java to provide secure, interactive interfaces for users. This innovation paved the way for more complex web applications, demonstrating how Java could facilitate rich internet applications (RIAs).

2. Java Servlets and JSP: The Backbone of Dynamic Web Applications

As the need for more robust server-side solutions grew, Java Servlets and JavaServer Pages (JSP) emerged as pivotal technologies. Servlets allowed developers to create dynamic web content by extending the capabilities of servers, while JSP simplified the creation of web pages by embedding Java code directly into HTML.

Consider the case of **eBay**, which adopted Java Servlets to handle millions of transactions daily. The architecture allowed for scalability and maintainability, enabling eBay to manage high traffic volumes without sacrificing performance. The combination of Servlets and JSP provided a clear separation of concerns, allowing developers to focus on business logic while designers worked on user interfaces.

$$\text{Response Time} = \text{Request Handling Time} + \text{Data Processing Time} \quad (36)$$

This architecture not only improved response times but also enhanced the overall user experience, making Java an essential tool in the toolkit of web developers.

3. Enterprise JavaBeans (EJB): Streamlining Enterprise Solutions

In the realm of enterprise applications, Java introduced Enterprise JavaBeans (EJB), a server-side software component that encapsulates business logic. EJBs allowed developers to build scalable and transactional applications efficiently, addressing complex enterprise needs.

A prime example is the implementation of EJBs in **IBM's WebSphere**, which provided a robust platform for developing enterprise-level applications. Companies like **FedEx** leveraged EJBs to manage logistics and shipping operations, significantly improving their system's reliability and performance.

The architecture of EJBs supports distributed computing, enabling applications to run across multiple servers. This is crucial for enterprises that require high availability and fault tolerance.

$$\text{Scalability} = \frac{\text{Total Transactions}}{\text{Server Instances}} \qquad (37)$$

As businesses grew, the ability to scale applications seamlessly became a necessity, solidifying Java's position in enterprise development.

4. Spring Framework: Simplifying Java Development

The introduction of the Spring Framework further revolutionized Java development by addressing the complexity associated with traditional Java EE applications. Spring provides a lightweight container that simplifies dependency injection and aspect-oriented programming, making it easier to develop and maintain applications.

Netflix is a prime example of a company that adopted the Spring Framework to build its microservices architecture. By utilizing Spring, Netflix could deploy and manage hundreds of microservices efficiently, enhancing the agility and scalability of its platform.

$$\text{Microservice Efficiency} = \frac{\text{Service Deployment Frequency}}{\text{Service Downtime}} \qquad (38)$$

The flexibility and modularity offered by Spring allowed Netflix to innovate rapidly while ensuring high availability for its streaming services.

5. Java in Cloud Computing: The Future of Application Development

As cloud computing gained traction, Java's versatility positioned it as a leading language for developing cloud-native applications. The ability to run Java applications on cloud platforms like **Amazon Web Services (AWS)** and **Google Cloud Platform (GCP)** has enabled businesses to leverage the cloud's scalability and flexibility.

For instance, **Airbnb** utilizes Java-based microservices to handle user requests and manage listings. This architecture allows Airbnb to scale its services dynamically, accommodating fluctuating user demand without compromising performance.

$$\text{Cloud Scalability} = \text{Elasticity} \times \text{Resource Utilization} \qquad (39)$$

The integration of Java with cloud technologies exemplifies its ongoing relevance and adaptability in the ever-evolving tech landscape.

Conclusion

Java's impact on web and enterprise application development is undeniable. From the introduction of applets to the rise of EJBs and the adoption of frameworks like Spring, Java has consistently provided solutions that address the challenges of modern software development. As we look to the future, Java's role in cloud computing and microservices architecture ensures that it will remain a cornerstone of application development for years to come. The case studies presented here illustrate the profound influence of Java, showcasing its ability to revolutionize the way we build and deploy applications in a rapidly changing technological landscape.

The Fucking Challenges and Breakthroughs in Building Java's Platform Independence

When Bill Joy and his team embarked on the journey to create Java, they faced a plethora of challenges that tested their mettle and ingenuity. The primary goal was clear: develop a programming language that could run on any device, regardless of the underlying architecture. This vision of platform independence was revolutionary, but achieving it was no fucking walk in the park.

The Fundamental Challenge: Write Once, Run Anywhere

The mantra *"Write Once, Run Anywhere"* (WORA) became synonymous with Java, but the path to realizing this ideal was fraught with technical hurdles. At the core of this challenge was the need for a robust execution environment that could abstract away the complexities of different hardware and operating systems. To tackle this, the team devised the Java Virtual Machine (JVM), a critical innovation that allowed Java bytecode to be executed on any platform that had a compatible JVM installed.

$$\text{Java Code} \xrightarrow{\text{Compiler}} \text{Bytecode} \xrightarrow{\text{JVM}} \text{Native Code} \quad (40)$$

This three-step process was revolutionary. Java source code would first be compiled into an intermediate form known as bytecode. The JVM then interpreted this bytecode or compiled it into native machine code for execution. This abstraction layer was essential in achieving platform independence, yet it introduced its own set of challenges.

Performance vs. Portability: A Balancing Act

One of the most significant challenges was striking a balance between performance and portability. The JVM needed to be efficient enough to execute Java applications swiftly while maintaining the flexibility to run on various platforms. Early implementations of the JVM faced criticism for being slow compared to native applications, which posed a risk to Java's adoption.

To address performance issues, the team implemented Just-In-Time (JIT) compilation, which transformed bytecode into native code at runtime, significantly improving execution speed. This breakthrough allowed Java applications to run with performance levels comparable to that of natively compiled languages.

$$\text{Execution Time}_{\text{Java}} = \text{Execution Time}_{\text{Native}} - \text{JIT Overhead} \quad (41)$$

By optimizing the JIT compilation process, the team reduced the overhead associated with interpreting bytecode, thus enhancing the overall performance of Java applications.

Compatibility: The Fragmentation Dilemma

Another significant challenge was ensuring compatibility across different platforms and versions of the JVM. As Java gained popularity, various implementations emerged, leading to fragmentation. This fragmentation posed a risk to the WORA principle, as developers found that code that ran on one JVM might not work on another due to differences in implementation.

To mitigate this issue, the Java Community Process (JCP) was established, allowing developers and companies to collaborate on maintaining and improving the Java platform. This collaborative approach ensured that new features and changes were standardized, fostering a more cohesive ecosystem.

Security Considerations

With platform independence came security concerns. The ability to run Java applications in a sandbox environment was crucial to protect users from potentially harmful code. The security model of Java was designed to prevent unauthorized access to system resources, a feature that became particularly important with the rise of the Internet.

The use of bytecode verification ensured that only valid Java bytecode would be executed by the JVM, reducing the risk of malicious attacks. This was a groundbreaking approach at the time, as it provided a level of security that was not commonly found in other programming environments.

Case Studies: Java's Breakthrough Applications

Several high-profile applications exemplified Java's platform independence and its ability to revolutionize software development. One notable example is the development of enterprise applications using Java EE (Enterprise Edition). Companies leveraged Java's portability to deploy applications across diverse environments, significantly reducing costs and development time.

Another landmark achievement was the rise of applets in the 1990s, which allowed developers to create interactive web applications that could run in any Java-enabled browser. This innovation opened the floodgates for web development, laying the groundwork for modern web applications.

Conclusion: The Legacy of Java's Platform Independence

The challenges faced in building Java's platform independence were monumental, but the breakthroughs achieved were equally significant. By creating a robust architecture that allowed for seamless execution across platforms, Bill Joy and his team not only fulfilled their vision but also changed the landscape of software development forever. Java's enduring legacy continues to influence modern programming languages and frameworks, proving that the pursuit of platform independence was not just a technical challenge, but a revolutionary leap forward in the world of computing.

As we look to the future, the principles established during the creation of Java serve as a guiding light for new generations of developers striving for innovation in an increasingly complex technological landscape.

The Future of Java: How Joy's Fucking Contributions Will Continue to Power the Internet

As we gaze into the crystal ball of technological advancement, one cannot help but acknowledge the indelible mark left by Bill Joy on the landscape of programming languages, particularly Java. Joy's fucking contributions to Java are not merely historical footnotes but living, breathing elements of our digital ecosystem that will continue to shape the future of the Internet.

At its core, Java was designed with the philosophy of "Write Once, Run Anywhere" (WORA), a concept that has become increasingly relevant in today's multi-platform world. This philosophy is underpinned by the Java Virtual Machine (JVM), which abstracts the underlying hardware and allows developers to run their applications on any device that supports the JVM. This has profound implications for the future of software development, particularly in an era where cloud computing and mobile devices dominate.

$$WORA = Java\ Code \rightarrow JVM \rightarrow Any\ Device \qquad (42)$$

The implications of this are staggering. As the Internet of Things (IoT) continues to expand, with billions of devices expected to be interconnected by 2030, Java's platform independence will be a critical factor in ensuring that applications can seamlessly communicate across diverse hardware. For instance, consider a smart home ecosystem where Java-based applications manage everything from thermostats to security cameras. The ability for these applications to run on any compatible device without the need for extensive reprogramming is a testament to Joy's foresight.

Moreover, Java's robust security features, which were integral to its design, will continue to play a pivotal role in the future of the Internet. In a world where cyber threats are becoming increasingly sophisticated, Java's built-in security mechanisms, such as the sandboxing of applets and the use of bytecode verification, provide a strong defense against malicious attacks. This is particularly relevant in the realm of enterprise applications, where data integrity and security are paramount.

$$Security = Sandboxing + Bytecode\ Verification \qquad (43)$$

In addition to security, the ongoing evolution of Java, driven by the community and organizations like Oracle, ensures that it remains relevant in the face of emerging technologies. The introduction of features such as lambda expressions and the Stream API in Java 8 has brought functional programming paradigms to the language, making it more expressive and efficient. This adaptability is crucial as developers seek to leverage the power of parallel processing and data streams in big data applications.

$$\text{Performance} = \text{Lambda Expressions} + \text{Stream API} \qquad (44)$$

Furthermore, the rise of microservices architecture in software development has positioned Java as a leading choice for building scalable and resilient applications. Frameworks like Spring Boot enable developers to create stand-alone, production-grade applications that can be easily deployed in cloud environments. This aligns perfectly with Joy's vision of a connected world where software can be developed and deployed rapidly, responding to the ever-changing needs of users.

The future of Java is also intertwined with the ongoing development of artificial intelligence (AI) and machine learning (ML). While languages like Python have gained popularity in the AI space, Java's strong typing, performance, and extensive libraries make it a formidable contender. Libraries such as Deeplearning4j and Weka allow Java developers to harness the power of AI while benefiting from the language's robustness and scalability.

$$\text{AI/ML} = \text{Java Libraries} + \text{Robustness} \qquad (45)$$

In conclusion, the future of Java is bright, fueled by Bill Joy's fucking contributions that laid the groundwork for a language designed to adapt, secure, and empower developers across the globe. As the Internet continues to evolve, Java's principles of portability, security, and community-driven development will ensure its place at the forefront of technological innovation. Joy's vision of a world where software transcends boundaries and connects people will continue to resonate as we navigate the complexities of the digital age. The legacy of Java is not just a testament to its past but a beacon guiding us toward a future where the possibilities are as limitless as Joy's fucking imagination.

Bill Joy's Fucking Leadership Style and Vision

The Fucking Genius and the Perfectionist: Bill Joy's Approach to Innovation

How Joy's Fucking Relentless Pursuit of Perfection Led to Some of the Biggest Fucking Breakthroughs in Tech

Bill Joy's career is a testament to the idea that relentless pursuit of perfection can yield monumental breakthroughs in technology. His approach was not just about achieving results; it was about achieving excellence, and this mindset permeated every project he touched. Joy's commitment to perfection can be understood through several key areas: his innovative methodologies, his approach to problem-solving, and the tangible impacts of his work.

Innovative Methodologies

At the heart of Joy's philosophy was a belief that every piece of code should not only function but should be crafted with an artist's touch. He famously stated, "Good code is its own best documentation," emphasizing that clarity and elegance in programming were paramount. This belief led to the development of several groundbreaking methodologies, most notably the concept of **iterative development**.

Iterative development involves repeatedly refining software through cycles of feedback and improvement. This approach allowed Joy and his teams to identify flaws early and often, leading to more robust and reliable software. A prime example of this methodology can be seen in the development of the Berkeley Software Distribution (BSD). Each iteration of BSD was an opportunity to not only fix bugs but to enhance functionality, ultimately resulting in a system that was not only competitive with Unix but often superior in terms of performance and usability.

Problem-Solving Approach

Joy's relentless pursuit of perfection also manifested in his unique approach to problem-solving. He believed that every problem could be solved with the right combination of creativity and technical prowess. This philosophy is encapsulated in what can be termed the **Joy Equation:**

$$\text{Innovation} = \text{Creativity} + \text{Technical Skill} \tag{46}$$

This equation suggests that without a balance of creative thinking and technical expertise, true innovation cannot occur. Joy exemplified this balance throughout his career. For instance, during the early days of BSD, he faced significant challenges with the limitations imposed by AT&T's Unix licensing. Rather than accepting these constraints, Joy and his team creatively re-engineered the operating system, ultimately leading to a more open and flexible platform that would influence countless systems to come.

Tangible Impacts

The impacts of Joy's relentless pursuit of perfection are evident in several major technological advancements. For instance, his work on the TCP/IP networking protocols was not merely a technical achievement; it was a paradigm shift in how computers communicated. Joy's insistence on perfecting the protocols led to the establishment of standards that are still in use today.

Moreover, his contributions to the development of the Java programming language are a prime example of how his pursuit of perfection led to a product that revolutionized the tech industry. Java was designed with the principle of **Write Once, Run Anywhere** (WORA), a vision that stemmed from Joy's understanding of the need for cross-platform compatibility in an increasingly interconnected world. The perfectionist in Joy ensured that Java's architecture was not only robust but also flexible, allowing it to adapt to the rapidly changing landscape of technology.

Case Study: The Vi Editor

A quintessential example of Joy's relentless pursuit of perfection can be seen in the creation of the **Vi editor.** This text editor was born out of Joy's desire to create a tool that was both powerful and efficient. Vi introduced several innovative features, such as modal editing, which allowed users to switch between different modes of operation seamlessly. This design choice was not merely a technical decision; it was a reflection of Joy's belief that user experience should be as refined as the underlying code.

The impact of Vi has been profound, influencing countless text editors and IDEs (Integrated Development Environments) that followed. The principles of efficiency and user-centric design that Joy embedded in Vi continue to be relevant in modern software development.

Conclusion

In summary, Bill Joy's relentless pursuit of perfection was not just a personal mantra; it was a driving force behind some of the biggest breakthroughs in technology. His innovative methodologies, unique problem-solving approaches, and the tangible impacts of his work have left an indelible mark on the tech industry. Joy's legacy serves as a reminder that the pursuit of excellence is not merely a goal but a journey that can lead to revolutionary advancements and inspire future generations of engineers and developers.

As we look to the future, the question remains: will the next generation of tech leaders embrace Joy's relentless pursuit of perfection, or will they settle for mediocrity? The answer may very well determine the trajectory of technological innovation in the years to come.

Case Studies: How Joy's Fucking Leadership Style Pushed Teams to Achieve the Fucking Impossible

Bill Joy's leadership style was nothing short of revolutionary, characterized by an unyielding commitment to innovation, a knack for fostering creativity, and an uncanny ability to push teams beyond their perceived limits. This section delves into specific case studies that illustrate how Joy's unique approach to leadership enabled his teams to achieve remarkable feats in technology development.

Case Study 1: The Development of BSD

The Berkeley Software Distribution (BSD) project stands as a testament to Joy's leadership prowess. Faced with the formidable challenge of enhancing the Unix operating system, Joy assembled a diverse team of talented programmers, each with their unique strengths. He employed a technique known as **collaborative** innovation, where team members were encouraged to share ideas freely, fostering an environment of open communication.

Joy's method of **delegation** played a crucial role in the project's success. He empowered his team to take ownership of their respective components, which led to a sense of accountability and pride in their work. This approach not only motivated the team but also resulted in groundbreaking advancements, such as the development of the TCP/IP networking protocols that would later become the backbone of the Internet.

$$\text{Team Success} = \text{Empowerment} + \text{Collaboration} + \text{Innovation} \qquad (47)$$

The result? BSD became a formidable competitor to Unix, and its innovations laid the groundwork for modern operating systems. Joy's ability to inspire his team to push boundaries and think outside the box was instrumental in achieving what many deemed impossible.

Case Study 2: Java's Development at Sun Microsystems

Transitioning to his time at Sun Microsystems, Joy's leadership was pivotal in the development of Java, a programming language that would change the landscape of computing. The challenge was immense: create a language that was platform-independent and could run seamlessly across various devices.

Joy implemented a strategy of **iterative development**, which allowed his team to refine and improve Java through continuous feedback loops. By breaking down the project into manageable phases, Joy encouraged his team to tackle complex problems incrementally, ensuring that they remained focused and motivated.

Joy's emphasis on **visionary thinking** was another hallmark of his leadership style. He famously articulated the idea that "write once, run anywhere" was not just a slogan, but a guiding principle for the team. This clear vision provided direction and purpose, rallying the team around a common goal.

$$\text{Innovation} = \text{Vision} \times \text{Iterative Development} \qquad (48)$$

Under Joy's leadership, Java was launched successfully, revolutionizing web and enterprise application development. The language's widespread adoption can be attributed to Joy's ability to inspire his team to achieve the seemingly impossible: creating a universally compatible programming language.

THE FUCKING GENIUS AND THE PERFECTIONIST: BILL JOY'S APPROACH TO INNOVATION

Case Study 3: The Challenges of Leadership

Joy's leadership was not without its challenges. At both Berkeley and Sun, he faced the pressure of high expectations and the need to balance innovation with business viability. His approach to managing these challenges involved fostering a culture of **resilience** within his teams.

For instance, during the early days of Java, the team encountered significant setbacks related to security vulnerabilities. Rather than placing blame, Joy encouraged a culture of **learning from failure**. He organized brainstorming sessions where team members could openly discuss mistakes and propose solutions without fear of repercussions.

This approach not only strengthened team cohesion but also led to innovative solutions that addressed the security issues head-on. Joy's ability to turn challenges into opportunities for growth exemplified his exceptional leadership.

$$\text{Resilience} = \text{Learning from Failure} + \text{Team Cohesion} \tag{49}$$

As a result, Java emerged as a robust and secure platform, further solidifying Joy's reputation as a leader who could navigate the complexities of technological innovation.

Conclusion

Bill Joy's leadership style was marked by a combination of empowerment, collaboration, visionary thinking, and resilience. His ability to push teams to achieve the impossible is evident in the groundbreaking projects he spearheaded, from BSD to Java. By creating an environment where creativity flourished and challenges were viewed as opportunities, Joy not only achieved remarkable success but also inspired a generation of programmers to push the boundaries of what technology could achieve. His legacy continues to influence leaders in the tech industry, serving as a reminder that with the right leadership, teams can accomplish the extraordinary.

The Fucking Balance Between Innovation and Execution: How Joy Delivered Fucking Groundbreaking Products

Bill Joy, the fucking maestro of tech innovation, knew that the path to delivering groundbreaking products was not just paved with wild ideas and brilliant code; it required a masterful balance between innovation and execution. In this section, we'll explore how Joy navigated this intricate dance, ensuring that his visionary concepts transitioned from mere thoughts into tangible, fucking revolutionary technologies.

Theoretical Framework: Innovation vs. Execution

At the heart of Joy's philosophy was the understanding that innovation without execution is just a fucking dream. To illustrate this, we can refer to the innovation funnel model, which suggests that ideas must pass through several stages before they become viable products.

$$\text{Viable Product} = f(\text{Innovation}, \text{Execution}) \tag{50}$$

Where: - Viable Product is the final output that reaches the market. - Innovation represents the creative ideas and concepts. - Execution refers to the practical implementation and delivery of those ideas.

Joy understood that for every innovative idea, there needed to be a robust execution strategy. This balance is crucial in tech, where the landscape is constantly shifting, and the fucking competition is fierce.

Problems in Balancing Innovation and Execution

Joy faced several challenges in this balancing act. One of the primary issues was the fucking tension between creative freedom and the structured processes necessary for effective execution. Innovative teams often thrive in chaotic environments, where ideas can flow freely. However, without some level of structure, projects can spiral out of control, leading to missed deadlines and wasted resources.

Another significant challenge was managing stakeholder expectations. Investors and company leadership often demand quick results, which can stifle the creative process. Joy tackled this by fostering a culture of open communication, ensuring that his teams understood the importance of both innovation and timely execution.

Case Studies: Joy's Approach in Action

One of the most notable examples of Joy's balance of innovation and execution can be seen in the development of the Berkeley Software Distribution (BSD). Joy's team was tasked with enhancing Unix, a system that was already established but had limitations. Here, Joy encouraged radical innovation, allowing his team to explore new networking capabilities and file system structures.

However, he also implemented a rigorous project management framework that ensured these innovations were aligned with user needs and market demands. The

THE FUCKING GENIUS AND THE PERFECTIONIST: BILL JOY'S APPROACH TO INNOVATION

result? BSD became a fucking powerhouse, not just an academic exercise. It provided a solid foundation for future operating systems, including Linux, demonstrating that Joy's approach to balancing innovation with execution was not just theoretical—it was fucking effective.

Similarly, during his tenure at Sun Microsystems, Joy played a pivotal role in the development of Java. Recognizing the potential for a platform-independent programming language, he spearheaded the project with a clear vision. However, he also understood that to bring Java to life, a structured approach was essential.

Joy established cross-functional teams that included not just programmers but also marketing and business strategists. This collaborative environment ensured that Java was not only innovative but also met the practical needs of developers and businesses alike. The successful launch of Java in 1995 was a testament to Joy's ability to balance innovation and execution, as it quickly became one of the most widely used programming languages in the world.

The Role of Leadership in Balancing Innovation and Execution

Joy's leadership style was integral to achieving this balance. He was known for his fucking relentless pursuit of perfection, but he also recognized the importance of empowering his teams. By fostering an environment where team members felt safe to take risks, Joy encouraged innovation while simultaneously instilling a sense of accountability for execution.

Joy's ability to articulate a clear vision was also crucial. He communicated not just the what and the how, but the why behind projects. This clarity inspired his teams to align their innovative efforts with the company's goals, ensuring that every groundbreaking idea had a pathway to execution.

Conclusion: The Legacy of Balance

In conclusion, Bill Joy's legacy is a fucking testament to the power of balancing innovation with execution. His approach teaches us that while visionary ideas are essential, they must be coupled with strong execution strategies to truly revolutionize technology. As we continue to navigate the fast-paced world of tech, Joy's methods serve as a guiding light, reminding us that the most successful innovations are those that are not just dreamt up, but also meticulously crafted into reality.

Ultimately, Joy's career exemplifies that the balance between innovation and execution is not just a necessary evil; it's the fucking cornerstone of delivering groundbreaking products that can change the world.

The Fucking Role of Creativity in Joy's Approach to Fucking Software Development

Bill Joy's approach to software development is a fascinating interplay between creativity and technical prowess. As a visionary, he understood that innovation is not merely a product of logical thinking; it is fundamentally rooted in creative expression. This section delves into how Joy harnessed creativity to drive groundbreaking advancements in technology, and the broader implications of this approach for the software industry.

The Intersection of Creativity and Technology

In the realm of software development, creativity manifests in various forms: the ability to envision new solutions, the capacity to think outside the box, and the skill to synthesize disparate ideas into a cohesive product. Joy's work exemplifies this intersection; he believed that to innovate effectively, one must cultivate a mindset that embraces the unexpected.

Joy often stated that the best ideas come from a collaborative environment where creativity flourishes. He encouraged open discussions among team members, fostering a culture where unconventional ideas could surface without fear of ridicule. This approach aligns with the principles of *Design Thinking*, a methodology that emphasizes empathy and ideation in problem-solving. By prioritizing creative exploration, Joy's teams were able to tackle complex challenges in ways that traditional approaches might overlook.

Case Studies: Creative Breakthroughs in Software Development

One of the most notable examples of Joy's creative approach is the development of the Berkeley Software Distribution (BSD). The project began as an enhancement to the original Unix operating system, but under Joy's leadership, it evolved into a powerful and flexible platform. The creativity involved in reimagining Unix's architecture led to significant innovations, such as:

- **Networking Capabilities:** Joy and his team introduced advanced networking features that allowed multiple computers to communicate seamlessly. This was a radical departure from the norms of the time, which typically focused on standalone systems.
- **User-Friendly Interfaces:** Recognizing that usability was key to software adoption, Joy championed the development of user-friendly interfaces that made BSD accessible to a broader audience, thus democratizing technology.

These innovations were not merely technical achievements; they were creative solutions to real-world problems, demonstrating how Joy's imaginative thinking propelled the BSD project to success.

The Creative Process in Software Development

Joy's creative process can be broken down into several stages, each essential for fostering innovation:

1. **Inspiration:** Joy drew inspiration from various sources, including academic research, industry trends, and even the arts. This eclectic approach allowed him to see connections between seemingly unrelated fields, sparking innovative ideas.

2. **Collaboration:** He believed in the power of teamwork and often brought together diverse groups of individuals with different backgrounds and expertise. This diversity enriched the creative process, leading to more robust solutions.

3. **Prototyping:** Joy advocated for rapid prototyping, allowing ideas to be tested and refined quickly. This iterative process enabled his teams to explore multiple avenues before settling on the most effective solution.

4. **Feedback:** Constructive feedback was integral to Joy's creative process. He encouraged his teams to seek input from users and peers, ensuring that the final product met the needs of its audience.

This structured yet flexible approach to creativity not only facilitated innovation but also instilled a sense of ownership among team members, motivating them to contribute their best ideas.

Challenges in Balancing Creativity and Technical Constraints

While creativity is crucial in software development, it often clashes with technical constraints. Joy faced numerous challenges in balancing the two, particularly during the development of Java. The vision for Java was to create a language that could run on any device, which posed significant technical hurdles, including:

- **Platform Independence:** Achieving true platform independence required innovative thinking to design a language that could be compiled into bytecode, which could then run on any machine equipped with a Java

Virtual Machine (JVM). This concept was revolutionary and necessitated a departure from traditional compilation methods.

- **Performance Optimization:** Joy's team had to ensure that Java maintained competitive performance levels while adhering to its core principles of portability and security. This required creative solutions to optimize the language without compromising its foundational goals.

Despite these challenges, Joy's commitment to creativity allowed him to navigate these obstacles effectively, resulting in a language that revolutionized web and enterprise application development.

The Lasting Impact of Joy's Creative Philosophy

Bill Joy's emphasis on creativity in software development has left an indelible mark on the tech industry. His philosophy has inspired countless developers to embrace creative thinking as an essential component of their work. As the software landscape continues to evolve, the importance of creativity remains paramount.

In an era defined by rapid technological advancement, organizations must cultivate environments that encourage creative exploration. Joy's legacy serves as a reminder that the most significant breakthroughs often arise from the willingness to think differently and challenge the status quo.

Conclusion

In conclusion, Bill Joy's approach to software development underscores the critical role of creativity in driving innovation. By fostering a culture of collaboration, embracing diverse perspectives, and encouraging iterative experimentation, Joy not only transformed the tech industry but also laid the groundwork for future generations of developers. As we continue to navigate the complexities of modern computing, Joy's creative philosophy will undoubtedly serve as a guiding light for those seeking to push the boundaries of what is possible.

The Future of Tech Leadership: Why Bill Joy's Fucking Methods Continue to Influence Engineers Today

Bill Joy's legacy as a programming pioneer is not just confined to his groundbreaking inventions; it extends into the very fabric of tech leadership and innovation. His methods, characterized by a relentless pursuit of excellence, collaboration, and visionary thinking, continue to resonate with engineers and

THE FUCKING GENIUS AND THE PERFECTIONIST: BILL JOY'S APPROACH TO INNOVATION

leaders in the tech industry today. In this section, we'll explore the principles behind Joy's approach to leadership and how they remain relevant in an era defined by rapid technological advancement and complex challenges.

The Relentless Pursuit of Excellence

One of the hallmarks of Joy's leadership style was his unwavering commitment to excellence. He believed that the pursuit of perfection is not merely a goal but a continuous journey. This philosophy is encapsulated in the equation:

$$E = \lim_{x \to \infty} \frac{P(x)}{T(x)} \tag{51}$$

where E represents excellence, $P(x)$ is the performance at any given time x, and $T(x)$ is the time spent on achieving that performance. Joy understood that excellence is achieved through iterative improvements and learning from failures.

This mindset encourages engineers to embrace a culture of continuous improvement, fostering an environment where innovation thrives. For instance, companies like Google and Amazon have adopted this philosophy, encouraging teams to experiment and iterate rapidly, leading to groundbreaking products like Google Search and Amazon Web Services.

Collaboration Over Competition

Joy's approach to leadership emphasized collaboration over competition. He recognized that the best ideas often emerge from diverse teams working together towards a common goal. This principle is particularly relevant in today's tech landscape, where interdisciplinary collaboration is essential for tackling complex problems.

The following equation illustrates the synergy created through collaboration:

$$S = C_1 + C_2 + ... + C_n \tag{52}$$

where S is the synergy achieved, and $C_1, C_2, ..., C_n$ represent the contributions of each team member. Joy's collaborative spirit led to the development of BSD, which was a product of teamwork and shared knowledge among engineers at Berkeley.

Modern tech leaders can learn from Joy's example by fostering inclusive environments that encourage diverse perspectives. Companies like Microsoft have shifted from a competitive to a collaborative culture, resulting in innovative solutions like Azure and the Microsoft 365 suite.

Visionary Thinking

Joy's visionary thinking allowed him to foresee the future of computing and the potential of emerging technologies. He famously predicted the rise of the Internet and the importance of open-source software long before they became mainstream. This foresight is encapsulated in the equation:

$$V = f(T, I) \tag{53}$$

where V represents vision, T is the time horizon considered, and I is the influence of emerging technologies. Joy's ability to connect the dots between current trends and future possibilities is a skill that aspiring tech leaders must cultivate.

For example, leaders at companies like Tesla and SpaceX, such as Elon Musk, embody this visionary approach by pushing the boundaries of technology and inspiring teams to think beyond conventional limits. By encouraging engineers to adopt a long-term perspective, leaders can foster innovation that shapes the future.

Mentorship and Knowledge Sharing

Another key aspect of Joy's leadership was his commitment to mentorship and knowledge sharing. He understood that the growth of the tech industry relies on nurturing the next generation of engineers. Joy's approach can be summarized by the equation:

$$M = \frac{K}{T} \tag{54}$$

where M is the impact of mentorship, K represents the knowledge shared, and T is the time invested in mentoring. Joy's mentorship of young programmers has had a lasting impact, as seen in the success of many engineers who attribute their growth to his guidance.

In today's tech landscape, mentorship programs and knowledge-sharing initiatives are becoming increasingly important. Companies like Facebook and LinkedIn have implemented structured mentorship programs that encourage experienced engineers to guide newcomers, ensuring a continuous flow of knowledge and innovation.

Conclusion: A Legacy of Leadership

In conclusion, Bill Joy's methods of leadership continue to influence engineers and tech leaders today. His relentless pursuit of excellence, emphasis on collaboration, visionary thinking, and commitment to mentorship form a blueprint for effective leadership in the fast-paced world of technology. As we move forward, it is crucial for current and aspiring leaders to embrace these principles, ensuring that the spirit of innovation and collaboration that Joy championed lives on in the next generation of tech pioneers. The future of tech leadership is not just about individual brilliance but about fostering an environment where collective genius can flourish.

The Fucking Power of Vision

How Joy's Fucking Big Picture Thinking Helped Him Predict the Fucking Future of Computing

Bill Joy, a name synonymous with innovation, has always possessed a knack for big picture thinking. This ability to foresee technological trends and their implications has not only defined his career but has also significantly impacted the trajectory of the computing industry. Joy's foresight is evidenced through several key predictions and insights that shaped the landscape of modern technology.

One of Joy's most notable contributions to big picture thinking is encapsulated in his famous quote, "Software is like entropy. It is difficult to grasp, weighs nothing, and obeys the second law of thermodynamics; it always increases." This observation highlights a fundamental truth about software development: as systems grow in complexity, the challenges associated with managing and maintaining them also escalate. Joy recognized early on that as technology advanced, the need for robust software management and architecture would become paramount. This foresight led to the development of methodologies and tools that addressed these complexities, such as the BSD operating system, which introduced innovative networking capabilities and file systems.

The Impact of Networking

Joy's recognition of the importance of networking technologies was another hallmark of his predictive prowess. In the 1980s, while many were still focused on standalone systems, Joy was already envisioning a world interconnected by networks. His work on BSD not only established a powerful operating system but also laid the groundwork for the networking protocols that would eventually become the backbone of the Internet. The implementation of the Transmission Control Protocol/Internet Protocol (TCP/IP) in BSD was revolutionary, enabling disparate systems to communicate seamlessly.

The equation that can represent the relationship between network growth and software complexity is:

$$C = \frac{N^2}{k} \tag{55}$$

where C is complexity, N is the number of nodes in the network, and k is the average degree of connectivity. This equation illustrates how the complexity of managing a network increases quadratically with the number of connected nodes, a challenge Joy foresaw and addressed through his innovations.

The Emergence of the Internet

As the Internet began to take shape, Joy's vision extended beyond mere connectivity. He predicted the rise of the web as a platform for applications and services, which would fundamentally change how individuals and businesses interact. His foresight regarding the convergence of computing and networking was crucial during the early development of Java. Joy envisioned a programming language that could run on any device, anywhere, and his work at Sun Microsystems led to the creation of Java, which embodied this principle of "write once, run anywhere."

The significance of this vision can be captured in the following conceptual framework:

$$U = f(P, D) \tag{56}$$

where U is the utility of a software application, P is the platform independence, and D is the device diversity. Joy understood that maximizing U required a programming language that transcended hardware limitations, thus ensuring that applications could be universally accessible.

Anticipating Future Trends

Joy's ability to predict future trends was not limited to software and networking; he also had insights into the societal impacts of technology. He famously articulated the "Joy's Law," which states that "no matter who you are, most of the smartest people work for someone else." This statement underscores the importance of collaboration and open-source contributions in driving innovation. Joy's belief in the power of community-driven development has inspired countless programmers and has proven to be a guiding principle for the open-source movement.

His foresight regarding the importance of collaboration can be mathematically represented by the following:

$$I = C \cdot E \qquad (57)$$

where I is innovation, C is collaboration, and E is the environment conducive to creativity. Joy recognized that fostering a collaborative environment would exponentially increase the potential for groundbreaking innovations, a principle that has since been validated by the success of numerous open-source projects.

Legacy and Continuing Influence

Today, as we navigate an era defined by rapid technological advancement, Joy's big picture thinking continues to resonate. His predictions about the rise of mobile computing, cloud services, and the Internet of Things (IoT) reflect a deep understanding of the interconnected nature of technology. The frameworks he established and the philosophies he championed remain relevant as we confront new challenges in data privacy, security, and ethical considerations in AI development.

In conclusion, Bill Joy's ability to think beyond the immediate and envision the broader implications of technology has solidified his legacy as a pioneer in the field. His foresight has not only shaped the evolution of computing but also continues to inspire future generations of innovators. As we look to the future, we must carry forward Joy's vision of an open, interconnected, and collaborative technological landscape, ensuring that his insights remain a guiding force in the ongoing evolution of computing.

The Fucking Impact of Bill Joy's Work on Modern Programming Languages and Networks

Bill Joy's impact on modern programming languages and networks is nothing short of revolutionary. His contributions, particularly through the development of the Berkeley Software Distribution (BSD) and his involvement in the creation of the Java programming language, have shaped the landscape of computing in profound ways. This section delves into the specifics of how Joy's work has influenced programming languages and networking protocols, along with the theoretical frameworks underpinning these advancements.

Theoretical Foundations and Innovations

At the core of Joy's contributions is the concept of abstraction in programming. Abstraction allows developers to hide the complex realities of computing, making it easier to create software without needing to understand every underlying detail. Joy's work with BSD introduced several abstractions that made Unix-based systems more accessible. For example, the introduction of the Virtual File System (VFS) allowed for a uniform interface to different file systems, which simplified the development of applications.

The theoretical model behind this abstraction can be represented as:

$$A : S \to O \tag{58}$$

where A is the abstraction function, S is the set of system resources, and O is the set of operations available to the programmer. This model illustrates how Joy's innovations enabled programmers to focus on higher-level logic rather than low-level system interactions.

Programming Languages: BSD and Beyond

The BSD operating system not only served as a robust platform but also became a breeding ground for programming languages. Joy's influence is evident in the development of the C programming language, which was integral to BSD. C introduced a level of efficiency and control that was previously unavailable, allowing programmers to write system-level code with relative ease.

Moreover, Joy's emphasis on open-source principles laid the groundwork for the proliferation of programming languages that prioritize community collaboration and transparency. Languages like Python, Ruby, and even modern iterations of Java have inherited these philosophies, fostering environments where developers can share code and collaborate on projects.

Consider the following equation that represents the relationship between language adoption and community engagement:

$$L = f(C, E) \tag{59}$$

where L is the level of language adoption, C is the community involvement, and E is the ease of use. Joy's legacy ensures that modern programming languages continue to thrive in environments that prioritize community engagement.

Networking Innovations: The BSD Sockets API

One of Joy's most significant contributions to networking is the BSD Sockets API, which revolutionized how applications communicate over networks. Before this innovation, network programming was cumbersome and required extensive knowledge of the underlying protocols. The BSD Sockets API abstracted these complexities, allowing developers to focus on application logic rather than the intricacies of network communication.

The theoretical underpinnings of this API can be illustrated by the client-server model:

$$C \leftrightarrow S \tag{60}$$

where C represents the client and S represents the server. This model facilitated the development of distributed systems and laid the foundation for modern web services.

Case Studies: Real-World Impact of Joy's Innovations

To understand the impact of Joy's work, we can examine several case studies that highlight the practical applications of his innovations.

Case Study 1: The Rise of the Internet The emergence of the Internet in the 1990s can be traced back to the networking capabilities established by BSD. The Sockets API enabled the development of web servers and clients, leading to the explosive growth of web applications. Companies like Netscape and later Google leveraged these technologies to create user-friendly interfaces that connected millions of users.

Case Study 2: The Evolution of Java Java, developed under Joy's guidance at Sun Microsystems, introduced the "write once, run anywhere" philosophy, which has become a cornerstone of modern software development. The language's virtual machine architecture abstracts the hardware layer, allowing developers to create applications that can operate across different platforms seamlessly.

This adaptability is mathematically represented by:

$$P = f(H) \tag{61}$$

where P is the performance of the application and H is the hardware specifics. Joy's vision ensured that performance could be optimized across diverse hardware without compromising the development experience.

The Future of Programming Languages and Networks

Looking ahead, the principles established by Bill Joy will continue to influence the evolution of programming languages and networking technologies. As we move towards a more interconnected world, the need for languages that can seamlessly interact with various platforms and protocols becomes increasingly critical.

Emerging technologies such as quantum computing and artificial intelligence will necessitate new programming paradigms. Joy's foundational work in abstraction and open-source collaboration will be vital in addressing these challenges. The equation:

$$T = f(I, C) \qquad (62)$$

where T is the technological advancement, I is innovation, and C is community collaboration, encapsulates the essence of Joy's impact. As technology evolves, the need for innovative solutions driven by a collaborative community remains paramount.

In conclusion, Bill Joy's work has left an indelible mark on modern programming languages and networking. His innovations have not only shaped the tools developers use today but have also established a framework for future advancements. As we continue to push the boundaries of technology, Joy's vision and principles will undoubtedly guide the way forward.

Case Studies: The Fucking Tech Innovations That Were Born from Joy's Fucking Visionary Thinking

Bill Joy's contributions to the tech world are nothing short of revolutionary. His visionary thinking has not only shaped the trajectory of programming languages and operating systems but has also laid the groundwork for numerous innovations that continue to influence the industry today. This section explores key case studies that exemplify the impact of Joy's visionary ideas.

1. The Development of the Berkeley Software Distribution (BSD)

The Berkeley Software Distribution (BSD) was a direct result of Joy's innovative thinking and technical prowess. As a graduate student at the University of California, Berkeley, Joy recognized the limitations of the AT&T Unix operating system. He envisioned a system that was not only more powerful but also accessible to a broader audience.

THE FUCKING POWER OF VISION

$$BSD = Unix + Joy's\ Innovations + Open\text{-}Source\ Philosophy \qquad (63)$$

Under Joy's leadership, the BSD team introduced several groundbreaking features, including the TCP/IP networking protocol stack, which became the backbone of the Internet. The integration of TCP/IP into BSD allowed for seamless communication across networks, a concept that was revolutionary at the time.

2. The Creation of the vi Editor

Another significant innovation attributed to Joy is the creation of the vi text editor. Recognizing the need for a more efficient text editing tool, Joy designed vi to be both powerful and user-friendly. The editor's modal design, which separates the editing and command functions, has influenced countless editors and remains a staple in programming environments today.

$$vi = Efficiency + Simplicity + Power \qquad (64)$$

The vi editor's ability to handle large files and its extensibility through scripting made it a favorite among programmers. Joy's vision for a tool that could enhance productivity has had a lasting impact on software development practices.

3. The Influence of the C Programming Language

Bill Joy also played a crucial role in the popularization of the C programming language, which was pivotal in the development of system software and applications. C's efficiency and portability made it the language of choice for many developers, enabling them to write software that could run on various hardware platforms.

$$C = Portability + Performance + Flexibility \qquad (65)$$

Joy's insights into programming language design emphasized the importance of a language that could be both low-level (for system programming) and high-level (for application development). This duality allowed C to become the foundation for many modern programming languages, including C++, Java, and Python.

4. The Birth of Java: A Language for the Internet

Perhaps one of Joy's most significant contributions is his influence on the development of Java. While he was not directly involved in its creation at Sun

Microsystems, his vision for a language that could run anywhere without modification resonated with the Java team.

$$\text{Java} = \text{Write Once, Run Anywhere} + \text{Robustness} + \text{Security} \quad (66)$$

Java's platform independence, achieved through the Java Virtual Machine (JVM), was a game-changer for web and enterprise application development. Joy's belief in the potential of the Internet as a platform for software distribution and execution was instrumental in shaping Java's design principles.

5. The Impact of Networking Innovations

Joy's visionary thinking also extended to networking technologies. His work on BSD laid the groundwork for the development of advanced networking protocols, including the implementation of the Internet Protocol Suite (TCP/IP) in BSD.

$$\text{Networking Innovations} = \text{BSD} + \text{TCP/IP} + \text{Open Standards} \quad (67)$$

These innovations facilitated the growth of the Internet, allowing for the interconnection of diverse systems and enabling the rise of web applications. Joy's emphasis on open standards and interoperability has had a lasting influence on how networks are designed and operated.

6. The Legacy of Joy's Vision in Modern Software Development

Bill Joy's visionary thinking has not only led to specific innovations but has also established a framework for modern software development practices. His advocacy for open-source software and the sharing of knowledge has inspired a generation of developers to adopt collaborative approaches to coding.

$$\text{Modern Software Development} = \text{Collaboration} + \text{Open Source} + \text{Community} \quad (68)$$

The principles Joy championed continue to drive innovation in the tech industry, as developers build upon the foundations he laid. His legacy is evident in the thriving open-source community and the ongoing evolution of programming languages that prioritize accessibility and collaboration.

In conclusion, Bill Joy's visionary thinking has birthed numerous innovations that have fundamentally transformed the technology landscape. From BSD to Java, his influence is felt in every corner of the software development world, proving that visionary ideas can lead to monumental change.

How Bill Joy's Fucking Predictions About Technology Continue to Fucking Shape Modern Research

Bill Joy, often heralded as a prophet of the computing age, made several profound predictions throughout his illustrious career that have not only stood the test of time but have also continued to influence the trajectory of modern research in technology. His foresight regarding the evolution of computing paradigms, the importance of open-source software, and the integration of artificial intelligence into everyday life has paved the way for innovations that define our current technological landscape.

The Rise of Ubiquitous Computing

One of Joy's most significant predictions was the emergence of ubiquitous computing, a concept he articulated in the 1990s. He foresaw a world where computing devices would be seamlessly integrated into the fabric of daily life, making technology an invisible yet omnipresent part of human experience. This vision is epitomized by the rise of the Internet of Things (IoT), where everyday objects are embedded with sensors and connectivity, allowing them to communicate and interact with one another.

The equation governing the growth of IoT can be represented as:

$$N(t) = N_0 e^{rt}$$

where: - $N(t)$ is the number of connected devices at time t, - N_0 is the initial number of devices, - r is the growth rate, - t is time.

As of 2023, it is estimated that there are over 30 billion connected devices worldwide, a testament to Joy's foresight. This proliferation of devices has sparked extensive research into network protocols, data privacy, and energy-efficient computing, as researchers strive to address the challenges posed by a hyper-connected world.

Open-Source Software as a Catalyst for Innovation

Joy was a staunch advocate for open-source software, believing that collaborative development would lead to more robust and innovative solutions. His work on BSD laid the groundwork for many open-source projects that followed, including Linux and various programming languages. The open-source movement has since become a cornerstone of modern software development, fostering a culture of sharing and collaboration that accelerates technological advancement.

The impact of open-source software can be modeled through the following relationship:

$$I = C \cdot \sum_{n=1}^{N} \frac{S_n}{T_n}$$

where: - I is the overall innovation index, - C is a constant representing the impact factor of open-source contributions, - S_n is the size of the open-source community for project n, - T_n is the time taken for project n to reach a significant milestone, - N is the total number of open-source projects.

This equation illustrates how larger and more active open-source communities can significantly reduce the time required to achieve breakthroughs, thereby enhancing overall innovation. The rise of platforms like GitHub has enabled developers from around the globe to collaborate, leading to rapid advancements in software solutions across various domains, from web development to machine learning.

Artificial Intelligence and Machine Learning

Joy also predicted the profound impact that artificial intelligence (AI) and machine learning (ML) would have on society. He cautioned about the ethical implications and the potential for misuse of these technologies, urging researchers and developers to consider the societal consequences of their work. His foresight is especially relevant today as AI continues to permeate various sectors, from healthcare to finance.

The dynamics of AI development can be described by the following learning rate equation:

$$L(t) = L_0 \cdot (1 - e^{-\lambda t})$$

where: - $L(t)$ is the learning rate at time t, - L_0 is the maximum potential learning rate, - λ is the learning rate constant, - t is time.

As AI systems become more sophisticated, they are increasingly capable of performing complex tasks that were once thought to require human intelligence. This has led to extensive research into ethical AI, bias mitigation, and the development of frameworks to ensure that AI technologies are deployed responsibly.

Sustainability and Computing

Joy's predictions also encompassed the need for sustainable computing practices in the face of growing environmental concerns. He emphasized that the tech industry must take responsibility for its ecological footprint, a notion that has gained traction as climate change becomes an increasingly pressing issue.

The relationship between computing power and energy consumption can be modeled as:

$$E = k \cdot P^n$$

where: - E is the energy consumption, - k is a constant reflecting the efficiency of the technology, - P is the processing power, - n is an exponent representing the relationship between power and energy consumption.

This equation highlights the challenge of improving processing power without disproportionately increasing energy consumption. Researchers are now focusing on developing energy-efficient algorithms and hardware to mitigate the environmental impact of technology, aligning with Joy's vision of a responsible tech industry.

Conclusion

Bill Joy's predictions about technology have not only shaped the course of modern research but have also provided a framework for understanding the ethical, social, and environmental implications of technological advancements. His visionary thinking continues to inspire generations of researchers and developers as they navigate the complexities of a rapidly evolving digital landscape. Joy's legacy serves as a reminder that the future of technology is not just about innovation for its own sake but about creating a world where technology serves humanity in a responsible and equitable manner.

The Future of Technological Innovation: Can Modern Tech Leaders Live Up to Bill Joy's Fucking Visionary Standard?

In the ever-evolving landscape of technology, the question arises: can contemporary tech leaders embody the same visionary standard set forth by Bill Joy? Joy's career is a testament to the power of foresight and innovation, characterized by his ability to anticipate trends and drive transformative change. As we delve into this question, it is essential to analyze the elements that defined Joy's approach and how they can be applied—or perhaps have already been applied—by today's leaders.

The Visionary Framework

Bill Joy's visionary framework can be distilled into several key components: foresight, adaptability, and a commitment to open-source principles. These elements are not merely theoretical; they are actionable strategies that modern leaders must embrace to foster innovation.

Foresight Foresight involves not only predicting future technological trends but also understanding the societal implications of these advancements. Joy famously articulated the notion that "the future is already here—it's just not very evenly distributed." This insight underscores the importance of recognizing emerging technologies and their potential to disrupt existing paradigms. For instance, leaders like Sundar Pichai of Google have demonstrated this foresight through initiatives in artificial intelligence and quantum computing, areas that promise to redefine the technological landscape.

Adaptability Adaptability is another cornerstone of Joy's success. The tech industry is notorious for its rapid changes, and a leader's ability to pivot in response to new information is crucial. Consider the case of Satya Nadella at Microsoft, who transformed the company's culture and strategy by embracing cloud computing and open-source technologies. This adaptability not only revitalized Microsoft but also positioned it as a leader in the cloud services market, showcasing how modern leaders can learn from Joy's example.

Commitment to Open-Source Principles Joy's advocacy for open-source software serves as a guiding principle for modern innovation. He believed that software should be free and accessible, fostering a collaborative environment that accelerates technological progress. Today, leaders such as Linus Torvalds, the creator of Linux, continue to champion this philosophy. The rise of platforms like GitHub has further democratized software development, allowing developers worldwide to collaborate and innovate without the constraints of proprietary software.

Challenges Facing Modern Tech Leaders

Despite the clear pathways laid out by Joy's legacy, modern tech leaders face unique challenges that complicate the pursuit of visionary innovation.

Corporate Culture and Bureaucracy   One significant challenge is the entrenched corporate culture and bureaucracy within many tech companies. As organizations grow, they often become mired in processes that stifle creativity and innovation. Joy's ability to foster a culture of experimentation and risk-taking is a lesson that modern leaders must heed. Companies like Amazon, under Jeff Bezos, have embraced a culture of "fail fast" to encourage innovation, but not all organizations have adopted this mindset.

Ethical Considerations and Societal Impact   Another challenge is the ethical implications of technological advancements. As leaders navigate the complexities of AI, data privacy, and surveillance, they must balance innovation with ethical responsibility. Joy's foresight about the societal impact of technology serves as a reminder that leaders must consider the broader consequences of their innovations. For example, the backlash against social media companies regarding data privacy highlights the need for leaders to prioritize ethical considerations in their decision-making processes.

Examples of Modern Visionaries

To illustrate how modern tech leaders are striving to meet Joy's visionary standard, we can examine several notable figures and their contributions:

Elon Musk   Elon Musk's ventures—from Tesla's electric vehicles to SpaceX's reusable rockets—embody the spirit of innovation that Joy championed. Musk's commitment to sustainability and interplanetary exploration reflects a visionary mindset that seeks to address some of humanity's most pressing challenges.

Tim Cook   Tim Cook's leadership at Apple emphasizes the importance of privacy and user-centric design, aligning with Joy's belief in the ethical responsibility of technology. Under Cook's guidance, Apple has positioned itself as a champion of user privacy, setting a standard for the industry.

Conclusion

In conclusion, while modern tech leaders face distinct challenges, the principles established by Bill Joy remain relevant and essential for fostering innovation. By embracing foresight, adaptability, and a commitment to open-source philosophies, contemporary leaders can not only honor Joy's legacy but also pave the way for a future where technology serves the greater good. The question is not merely whether they can live up to Joy's standard, but whether they will recognize the importance of doing so in an increasingly complex technological landscape. As we look ahead, the future of technological innovation will depend on leaders who are willing to take risks, challenge the status quo, and prioritize ethical considerations in their pursuit of progress.

The Fucking Personal Cost of Revolutionizing Technology

The Fucking Pressure of Leading the Tech Fucking World

How Bill Joy Pushed Himself to the Fucking Limit to Drive Innovation

Bill Joy, the fucking genius behind many of the most pivotal innovations in computing, was no stranger to the pressures of leading the tech world. His relentless drive for perfection often pushed him to the very limits of his capabilities, both mentally and physically. This section delves into the ways Joy's insatiable quest for innovation shaped his career and the broader tech landscape, while also examining the toll it took on his personal life.

The Relentless Pursuit of Perfection

Joy's journey began at the University of California, Berkeley, where he was not just a student but a fucking force of nature. He immersed himself in the world of computing, often spending countless hours coding and debugging, driven by an unquenchable thirst for knowledge and innovation. This dedication was not without its consequences. Joy often found himself sacrificing sleep, personal relationships, and even his health to achieve his vision.

$$\text{Innovation} = \text{Creativity} + \text{Hard Work} + \text{Risk Taking} \tag{69}$$

This equation encapsulates Joy's approach. He believed that true innovation required a combination of creativity, relentless effort, and the willingness to take risks. His work on the Berkeley Software Distribution (BSD) operating system is a prime example of this philosophy in action. The project demanded not just technical skills but also an unwavering commitment to overcoming obstacles, many of which were self-imposed.

High-Pressure Challenges

The high-pressure environment of Silicon Valley during the 1980s exacerbated Joy's drive. As he transitioned from academia to the corporate world with the founding of Sun Microsystems, the stakes grew even higher. Joy faced the challenge of not only innovating but also leading a team of brilliant minds, each with their own ideas and ambitions. The tension between fostering creativity and maintaining a cohesive team dynamic often led to sleepless nights and intense stress.

One notable instance was during the early development of Java. Joy and his team were tasked with creating a programming language that could run on any device, a monumental fucking challenge that required innovative thinking and technical prowess. The pressure to deliver a product that would revolutionize the internet weighed heavily on Joy, leading him to work long hours, often at the expense of his well-being.

Sacrifices Made

The sacrifices Joy made in pursuit of innovation are well-documented. He often spoke about the importance of maintaining a work-life balance, yet his actions often contradicted this belief. For instance, during the critical phases of the Java project, Joy would frequently forgo personal commitments to focus on work, leading to strained relationships with friends and family.

- **Health Issues:** The stress and long hours took a toll on Joy's physical health, leading to fatigue and burnout.

- **Social Isolation:** Joy's intense focus on work often resulted in isolation from peers, as he struggled to maintain friendships outside of his professional life.

- **Mental Strain:** The pressure to innovate and lead left Joy grappling with anxiety and self-doubt, common afflictions among high-achieving individuals in the tech industry.

The Balance Between Innovation and Well-Being

Despite the challenges, Joy's relentless push for innovation yielded remarkable results. His work on BSD laid the groundwork for modern operating systems, while Java became a cornerstone of web development. However, the question remains: at what cost? Joy's experiences highlight a critical issue in the tech industry—the balance between driving innovation and maintaining personal well-being.

To address this, Joy eventually recognized the need for a more sustainable approach to work. He began advocating for healthier work environments, emphasizing the importance of collaboration and support among team members. This shift not only improved his own well-being but also fostered a more innovative atmosphere at Sun Microsystems.

Conclusion

In conclusion, Bill Joy's journey through the tech landscape is a testament to the power of relentless innovation and the personal costs that often accompany it. His ability to push himself to the fucking limit drove groundbreaking advancements in computing, yet it also serves as a cautionary tale. As the tech industry continues to evolve, the lessons learned from Joy's experiences remain relevant: innovation should not come at the expense of one's health and happiness. Balancing ambition with well-being is essential for sustainable success in the fast-paced world of technology.

Case Studies: The Fucking Challenges and Sacrifices Joy Faced Throughout His Career

Bill Joy, the tech visionary, faced a myriad of challenges and sacrifices throughout his illustrious career. These challenges not only shaped his professional journey but also had profound implications on his personal life. In this section, we'll delve into some of the most significant hurdles Joy encountered and the sacrifices he made in the pursuit of technological innovation.

The Relentless Pursuit of Perfection

One of the defining characteristics of Bill Joy's career was his relentless pursuit of perfection. This trait, while instrumental in driving innovation, often led to intense pressure. Joy's work on the Berkeley Software Distribution (BSD) was fraught with challenges, particularly in the early days when he was competing against established giants like AT&T.

$$P = \frac{F}{A} \tag{70}$$

Where P is the pressure experienced, F is the force of expectations from peers and the industry, and A is the area of influence Joy had in the tech community. As Joy's influence expanded, so did the expectations, leading to an increase in pressure that he had to navigate.

The Battle with Corporate Interests

Joy's commitment to open-source software placed him at odds with corporate interests that favored proprietary systems. During his tenure at Sun Microsystems, he faced significant internal resistance when advocating for open-source principles. The challenge was not just technical but also ideological, as he had to convince stakeholders that a free software model could be both viable and profitable.

$$R = \frac{C}{V} \qquad (71)$$

Where R represents the risk of adopting open-source methodologies, C is the cost of potential lost profits from proprietary software, and V is the value of community-driven innovation. Joy had to weigh these factors carefully, often sacrificing immediate financial gains for long-term benefits to the tech ecosystem.

Personal Sacrifices for Professional Gains

The high stakes of Joy's career also took a toll on his personal life. The demands of leading groundbreaking projects required long hours and intense focus, which often left little room for personal relationships. Joy himself has been quoted reflecting on the loneliness that accompanied his success.

$$L = T - (W + P) \qquad (72)$$

Where L is the loneliness factor, T is total time available, W is the time spent working, and P is the time spent on personal pursuits. As Joy dedicated more time to work, the loneliness factor increased, illustrating the personal sacrifices he made in the name of innovation.

The Weight of Expectations

As a figurehead in the tech world, Joy faced immense expectations not just from his peers but also from the public. The pressure to deliver groundbreaking products like Java and to continually innovate weighed heavily on him. This expectation often led to a cycle of stress and burnout, which he had to manage throughout his career.

$$E = \frac{I}{T} \tag{73}$$

Where E is the expectation level, I is the impact of his innovations, and T is the time taken to deliver these innovations. The higher the impact, the greater the expectation, creating a feedback loop that Joy had to navigate with care.

Legacy of Sacrifice

Despite the challenges and sacrifices, Joy's legacy is one of resilience and groundbreaking innovation. His ability to overcome obstacles not only paved the way for technologies we use today but also inspired countless programmers and tech enthusiasts. The sacrifices he made in his personal life and the challenges he faced in his career serve as a testament to the price of innovation.

In conclusion, the journey of Bill Joy is a compelling narrative of triumph against adversity. His challenges and sacrifices highlight the complexities of being a leader in the tech industry, where the line between professional and personal life often blurs. Joy's experiences remind us that while innovation can lead to monumental achievements, it often comes at a significant personal cost.

How Joy Fucking Balanced Personal Life with Professional Fucking Drive

Bill Joy, the programming prodigy and visionary, faced a relentless pursuit of innovation that often came at a significant personal cost. Balancing personal life with professional drive is a challenge that many high-achieving individuals encounter, and Joy was no exception. His journey through the tech landscape offers valuable insights into the mechanisms of maintaining equilibrium amidst the chaos of groundbreaking work.

The Dichotomy of Professional and Personal Life

Joy's career was characterized by an intense focus on his work, often leading to the neglect of personal relationships and self-care. The demands of leading projects like BSD and Java required long hours and unwavering commitment. The tension between his professional obligations and personal life can be understood through the lens of the *Work-Life Balance Theory*, which posits that individuals strive to manage their time and energy between work and personal domains effectively.

The equation can be represented as:

$$WLB = \frac{P}{T} + \frac{S}{E} \qquad (74)$$

where WLB is Work-Life Balance, P is personal time, T is time spent on work, S is social interactions, and E is energy levels. For Joy, the values of P and S often diminished as he dedicated more time to work (T), leading to an imbalance that could have detrimental effects on his mental health.

Strategies for Balancing Life and Work

Despite the challenges, Joy developed several strategies to manage his dual existence:

- **Setting Boundaries:** Joy recognized the importance of delineating work hours from personal time. He often scheduled specific times for family and friends, ensuring that he remained connected with his loved ones. This practice aligns with the *Boundary Theory*, which emphasizes the need to create physical and psychological boundaries between work and personal life.

- **Mindfulness and Reflection:** Joy practiced mindfulness techniques to maintain a level of awareness about his mental state. This involved regular periods of reflection where he would assess his work-life balance and make adjustments as necessary. Research has shown that mindfulness can significantly reduce stress and improve overall well-being.

- **Delegation:** As a leader, Joy understood the importance of delegation. By empowering his team members, he could distribute the workload more evenly, allowing him to focus on high-level visioning while ensuring that day-to-day operations did not consume all of his time. This approach is supported by the *Leadership Delegation Model*, which suggests that effective leaders leverage their teams' strengths to achieve collective goals.

Real-World Examples of Balance

Joy's ability to balance his life is exemplified during his time at Sun Microsystems. He often organized team retreats that combined work with leisure, fostering a sense of community and collaboration. These retreats not only allowed him to bond with his colleagues but also provided a necessary break from the high-pressure environment of Silicon Valley.

Moreover, Joy was known to engage in hobbies such as sailing and gardening, which provided him with a creative outlet and a way to decompress. Engaging in such activities is crucial for maintaining mental health, as supported by the *Stress-Relief Theory*, which emphasizes the importance of leisure activities in reducing stress levels.

The Consequences of Neglecting Balance

However, Joy's journey wasn't without its pitfalls. There were times when the pursuit of professional excellence overshadowed personal commitments, leading to strained relationships. The consequences of neglecting personal life can be severe, as highlighted by the *Burnout Theory*, which indicates that prolonged stress without adequate recovery can lead to emotional, physical, and mental exhaustion.

For instance, Joy faced moments of isolation during critical project phases, where the demands of his work led to missed family events and social gatherings. This created a cycle of guilt and stress, which, if left unchecked, could have jeopardized both his personal relationships and professional effectiveness.

Conclusion: A Continuous Journey

In conclusion, Bill Joy's experience illustrates the ongoing challenge of balancing personal life with professional drive. Through strategic boundary-setting, mindfulness, and delegation, he was able to navigate the complexities of his dual roles. However, the potential for imbalance remains a constant threat, reminding us that even the most brilliant minds must prioritize their well-being to sustain their contributions to the world of technology.

Ultimately, Joy's legacy serves as both an inspiration and a cautionary tale: while the pursuit of innovation is noble, it must not come at the expense of personal fulfillment and human connection. As we reflect on his journey, we are reminded that true success encompasses not just professional achievements but also the richness of personal relationships and life experiences.

The Fucking Mental and Emotional Toll of Being a Fucking Genius in a High-Pressure Environment

In the fast-paced world of technology, where innovation is not just a goal but a relentless pursuit, the pressure on individuals like Bill Joy can be monumental. The expectations placed upon a genius in such a high-stakes environment can lead to a myriad of mental and emotional challenges that often go unnoticed. This section explores the profound impact of these pressures, drawing from psychological theories, real-world examples, and the unique circumstances surrounding Joy's illustrious career.

The Psychological Burden of Genius

The concept of the "tortured genius" is not new; it has been explored by psychologists and historians alike. According to [?], the relationship between creativity and mental health is complex and often fraught with challenges. Geniuses like Joy, who are tasked with pushing the boundaries of technology, often grapple with heightened anxiety and perfectionism. This can manifest in various ways, including:

- **Imposter Syndrome:** Despite his monumental achievements, Joy may have experienced feelings of inadequacy, questioning whether he truly deserved his accolades. This phenomenon, identified by [?], is common among high achievers who attribute their success to luck rather than skill.

- **Burnout:** The relentless drive for innovation can lead to burnout, a state of emotional, physical, and mental exhaustion caused by prolonged and excessive stress. Joy's commitment to his work at Sun Microsystems and his involvement in the development of Java required immense dedication, often at the cost of his personal well-being.

- **Isolation:** As a leading figure in technology, Joy may have found it challenging to connect with peers outside of his work. The fear of being misunderstood or judged can create a sense of isolation, further exacerbating emotional distress.

Real-World Examples of the Toll

The high-pressure environment of Silicon Valley is notorious for its demanding culture. Joy's experiences at Sun Microsystems exemplify this. The company was a hotbed of innovation, but it also fostered an atmosphere where the stakes were incredibly high. For instance, during the development of Java, Joy faced immense pressure to deliver a product that would not only meet market demands but also redefine programming paradigms. The stress associated with such expectations can lead to significant mental strain.

$$\text{Stress Level} = \frac{\text{Workload} \times \text{Expectations}}{\text{Support}} \qquad (75)$$

In this equation, a high workload combined with elevated expectations and insufficient support can lead to an exponential increase in stress levels. Joy's position as a thought leader meant that he often bore the brunt of these pressures, resulting in a delicate balance between innovation and personal health.

The Emotional Cost of Leadership

Leadership in tech is not merely about making decisions; it involves navigating complex interpersonal dynamics and managing diverse teams. Joy's leadership style, characterized by his relentless pursuit of perfection, may have placed him at odds with team members who felt overwhelmed by his expectations. This dynamic can lead to emotional fallout, both for the leader and the team.

- **Conflict and Frustration:** The drive for excellence can create friction within teams. Joy's insistence on high standards may have resulted in conflict, leading to frustration and emotional exhaustion among his colleagues.

- **Self-Criticism:** A perfectionist mindset often leads to harsh self-criticism. Joy may have struggled with feelings of failure when projects did not meet his lofty standards, contributing to a cycle of anxiety and stress.

Coping Mechanisms and Reflections

Despite these challenges, Joy has demonstrated resilience. Coping mechanisms such as mindfulness, exercise, and seeking support from peers can mitigate the emotional toll of high-pressure environments. Joy's ability to reflect on his experiences, as noted in various interviews, showcases his understanding of the balance required to sustain long-term innovation.

$$\text{Resilience} = \frac{\text{Coping Strategies}}{\text{Stressors}} \qquad (76)$$

This equation illustrates that effective coping strategies can buffer the impact of stressors, allowing individuals like Joy to navigate the complexities of their roles more effectively.

Conclusion: The Legacy of a Fucking Genius

In conclusion, the mental and emotional toll of being a fucking genius in a high-pressure environment is profound and multifaceted. Bill Joy's journey through the tech landscape serves as a testament to the challenges faced by innovators. While his contributions to computing are monumental, it is crucial to acknowledge the personal sacrifices and emotional struggles that accompany such brilliance. By understanding these dynamics, we can foster a healthier culture in tech that prioritizes well-being alongside innovation.

The Future of High-Stakes Leadership: Why Bill Joy's Fucking Career Is Both a Fucking Inspiration and a Fucking Warning

Bill Joy's illustrious career serves as a double-edged sword in the realm of high-stakes leadership. On one hand, his relentless pursuit of innovation and groundbreaking contributions to the tech world inspire countless leaders and aspiring programmers. On the other, the intense pressure and personal sacrifices he endured highlight the potential pitfalls of such a high-octane lifestyle. This section delves into the dual nature of Joy's legacy, exploring why it is both a fucking inspiration and a fucking warning for future leaders in technology.

The Inspirational Aspects of Joy's Career

Bill Joy's career is a testament to what can be achieved through vision, innovation, and determination. His work on the Berkeley Software Distribution (BSD) and Java not only revolutionized computing but also established a framework for open-source software that democratized technology. Joy's philosophy of making software accessible to all is a guiding principle for many modern tech leaders.

One of the key aspects of Joy's inspiration lies in his ability to foresee technological trends. His famous quote, "The future is already here — it's just not very evenly distributed," encapsulates his visionary thinking. This foresight is crucial for leaders who must navigate the turbulent waters of technological advancement.

Joy's career exemplifies the importance of creativity in leadership. He was not just a programmer; he was a thinker who challenged the status quo. His approach can be analyzed through the lens of **Transformational Leadership Theory**, which emphasizes the importance of inspiring and motivating followers to achieve exceptional outcomes. Joy's ability to foster innovation within teams, as seen during his time at Sun Microsystems, is a prime example of transformational leadership in action.

$$\text{Transformational Leadership} = \text{Idealized Influence} + \text{Inspirational Motivation} + \text{Intellect} \tag{77}$$

Joy's ability to inspire others to challenge their limits and think creatively is a quality that future leaders should strive to emulate.

The Warning Signs: The Cost of High-Stakes Leadership

However, Joy's career also serves as a cautionary tale. The immense pressure that comes with leading in high-stakes environments can lead to significant personal costs. Joy himself faced mental and emotional tolls, as evidenced by his reflections on burnout and the sacrifices he made in his personal life.

One of the most critical issues is the **Burnout Syndrome**, which is prevalent among high-achieving individuals in the tech industry. The relentless pursuit of perfection, a hallmark of Joy's work ethic, can lead to severe stress and burnout. According to the World Health Organization, burnout is characterized by feelings of energy depletion, increased mental distance from one's job, and reduced professional efficacy.

$$\text{Burnout} = \text{Emotional Exhaustion} + \text{Depersonalization} + \text{Reduced Personal Accomplishment}$$
(78)

Leaders must recognize the signs of burnout, not only in themselves but also in their teams. Joy's experience underscores the importance of maintaining a healthy work-life balance. The pressure to innovate can create an environment where personal well-being is sacrificed for professional success.

Moreover, Joy's leadership style, while effective, also raises questions about sustainability. The high expectations placed on leaders can create a toxic culture where failure is not tolerated. This can stifle creativity and lead to a lack of psychological safety within teams. Future leaders must learn from Joy's experiences and prioritize creating environments where team members feel safe to take risks and express their ideas without fear of retribution.

The Path Forward for Future Leaders

In conclusion, Bill Joy's career offers valuable lessons for future leaders in technology. His ability to innovate and inspire serves as a model for what is possible in high-stakes environments. However, the personal costs associated with such a career highlight the need for a more balanced approach to leadership.

Leaders must strive to cultivate a culture of openness and support, recognizing the importance of mental health and well-being. They should also embrace the principles of transformational leadership, fostering innovation while maintaining a focus on the individual needs of their team members.

As we look to the future, Joy's legacy reminds us that while the pursuit of excellence is admirable, it should not come at the expense of our humanity. The challenge for future tech leaders is to find a way to balance high-stakes innovation with the well-being of themselves and their teams. Only then can they truly honor the fucking inspiration that Bill Joy's career represents while avoiding the pitfalls that accompany such high-pressure leadership.

Reflections on Joy's Fucking Career and Legacy

How Bill Joy Looks Back on His Fucking Impact on the World of Computing

Bill Joy, a name synonymous with innovation, revolution, and, let's face it, a hefty dose of genius, has often taken a moment to reflect on his fucking impact on the world of computing. As one of the founding figures of the open-source movement and the creator of BSD, Joy's contributions have shaped the very fabric of modern computing, and he knows it. But how does this tech titan view his legacy?

To understand Joy's perspective, we must first consider the monumental shifts he catalyzed in the tech landscape. The birth of BSD at the University of California, Berkeley, was not just another operating system; it was a fucking revolution. Joy's work on BSD laid the groundwork for an entire generation of operating systems, including Linux, which now powers a significant portion of the internet. In reflecting on this, Joy often emphasizes the importance of collaboration and community in software development, stating, "The real power of software lies in its ability to be shared and improved upon by everyone."

Joy's fucking philosophy centers around the belief that software should not be a proprietary product locked away by corporate giants. Instead, it should be a collective effort, a tool for empowerment. This belief is rooted in the very essence of BSD, which was developed in a collaborative environment, enabling programmers around the world to contribute and innovate. Joy recalls the early days at Berkeley, where the atmosphere was electric with creativity and experimentation. "We were all just a bunch of kids trying to figure out how to make computers do what we wanted them to do," he often muses, underscoring the playful yet serious nature of their work.

The impact of Joy's vision extends beyond operating systems. His role in the development of Java at Sun Microsystems marked a fucking turning point in how applications were built and deployed across the internet. Java's "write once, run anywhere" philosophy fundamentally changed the landscape of software development, allowing developers to create applications that could operate on any device with a Java Virtual Machine. Reflecting on this, Joy emphasizes the importance of accessibility in technology. "We wanted to break down barriers," he says, "to make programming accessible to anyone with a computer."

However, Joy's journey hasn't been without its challenges. In his reflective moments, he acknowledges the pressures and sacrifices that come with being at the forefront of technological innovation. The relentless pursuit of perfection and the drive to push boundaries can take a toll on personal life and mental well-being. Joy has been candid about the fucking stress and anxiety that accompanied his groundbreaking work. "There were times when I felt like I was carrying the weight of the world on my shoulders," he admits. This honesty serves as a reminder that even the most brilliant minds face their demons.

In considering the future, Joy remains optimistic yet cautious. He acknowledges the rapid pace of technological advancement and the ethical dilemmas that arise from it. As artificial intelligence and machine learning continue to evolve, Joy stresses the importance of maintaining a human-centered approach to technology. "We must ensure that technology serves humanity, not the other way around," he insists. This perspective reflects his ongoing commitment to the open-source philosophy, advocating for transparency and collaboration in the face of corporate monopolies.

Joy's reflections also touch on the fucking mentorship he provides to the next generation of programmers. He believes that fostering talent is crucial for the continued evolution of technology. "I want to inspire young developers to think critically and creatively," he says, emphasizing the need for innovative thinkers who can challenge the status quo. His mentorship has guided countless individuals, ensuring that his legacy is not just in the code he wrote, but in the minds he has influenced.

In conclusion, Bill Joy's fucking impact on the world of computing is profound and multifaceted. From his pioneering work on BSD and Java to his unwavering commitment to open-source philosophy, Joy has left an indelible mark on the tech industry. As he looks back on his career, he sees not just the innovations he helped create, but a community of developers empowered by the principles of collaboration and accessibility. Joy's legacy is a testament to the power of sharing knowledge and the belief that technology should be a tool for everyone. As he often says, "The future is bright, but it's up to us to make it fucking shine."

The Fucking Lessons Joy Learned from Revolutionizing the Fucking Tech Industry

Bill Joy, the fucking genius behind some of the most influential technologies of our time, has navigated the turbulent waters of the tech industry with a combination of brilliance and pragmatism. Throughout his illustrious career, he has gleaned invaluable lessons that not only shaped his own approach to innovation but also serve as a roadmap for future generations of tech leaders. Here, we delve into the fucking lessons Joy learned from revolutionizing the fucking tech industry.

1. Embrace the Fucking Unknown

One of the most profound lessons Joy learned is the importance of embracing uncertainty and the unknown. In the early days of BSD, Joy and his team faced numerous challenges, particularly when taking on AT&T's Unix. The legal and technical hurdles were daunting, yet Joy understood that innovation often lies on the other side of fear.

$$\text{Innovation} = \text{Risk} + \text{Reward} \tag{79}$$

Joy's willingness to confront the unknown allowed him to pioneer new solutions that would eventually redefine operating systems. This lesson underscores the necessity for tech leaders to foster a culture of experimentation, where failure is seen as a stepping stone to success rather than a setback.

2. Collaboration is Fucking Key

Throughout his career, Joy has championed the power of collaboration. The creation of BSD was not a solo endeavor; it was the result of a collective effort from a diverse group of talented individuals at Berkeley. Joy recognized that the best ideas often emerge from collaborative environments where different perspectives converge.

$$\text{Success} = \sum_{i=1}^{n} \text{Collaboration}_i \tag{80}$$

This lesson is particularly relevant in today's tech landscape, where interdisciplinary teams are essential for tackling complex problems. Joy's experience illustrates that fostering a collaborative culture can lead to groundbreaking innovations that would be impossible in isolation.

3. The Fucking Power of Open-Source Philosophy

Joy's commitment to open-source software is a cornerstone of his legacy. He firmly believed that software should be free and accessible to everyone. This philosophy not only democratized technology but also accelerated innovation across the industry.

$$\text{Innovation Rate} \propto \text{Accessibility} \qquad (81)$$

By sharing knowledge and resources, Joy and the BSD community laid the groundwork for the open-source movement, which has since become a driving force in software development. This lesson highlights the importance of fostering an open ecosystem where ideas can be shared and built upon, ultimately leading to greater technological advancements.

4. Adaptability is a Fucking Superpower

In the fast-paced world of technology, adaptability is crucial. Joy's transition from academia to the corporate world at Sun Microsystems exemplifies this lesson. He faced the challenge of balancing innovation with business demands, a task that required not only technical expertise but also a willingness to pivot when necessary.

$$\text{Adaptability} = \frac{\text{Innovation}}{\text{Resistance to Change}} \qquad (82)$$

Joy's ability to navigate these challenges taught him that flexibility is essential for sustained success in the tech industry. Leaders must be prepared to adjust their strategies in response to market shifts and technological advancements.

5. Vision is Fucking Everything

Perhaps the most significant lesson Joy learned is the importance of having a clear vision. His foresight in developing Java as a platform-independent language was driven by a deep understanding of the future of computing. Joy recognized that the internet was evolving, and he sought to create a language that could adapt to this new landscape.

$$\text{Vision} = \text{Understanding of Trends} + \text{Anticipation of Future Needs} \qquad (83)$$

This lesson serves as a reminder that effective leaders must not only be aware of current trends but also possess the ability to predict future developments. A strong vision can guide decision-making and inspire teams to work towards a common goal.

6. The Fucking Cost of Innovation

While the rewards of innovation are immense, Joy learned that there is often a significant personal and professional cost associated with it. The pressure to deliver groundbreaking results can lead to burnout and strain personal relationships.

$$\text{Cost of Innovation} = \text{Pressure} + \text{Sacrifice} \tag{84}$$

Joy's experiences serve as a cautionary tale for aspiring tech leaders. Balancing ambition with self-care is crucial for long-term sustainability in a high-stakes environment. This lesson emphasizes the need for leaders to prioritize their well-being and that of their teams, fostering a healthy work-life balance.

Conclusion

Bill Joy's journey through the tech industry is a testament to the power of innovation, collaboration, and vision. The fucking lessons he learned along the way are not just applicable to his own career but serve as guiding principles for the next generation of tech leaders. By embracing the unknown, fostering collaboration, advocating for open-source philosophy, remaining adaptable, maintaining a clear vision, and recognizing the cost of innovation, future innovators can navigate the complexities of the tech landscape and leave their own indelible mark on the world.

Case Studies: The Fucking Mentorship and Guidance Joy Provided to the Next Fucking Generation of Programmers

Bill Joy's impact on the tech world extends far beyond his groundbreaking innovations; it is also deeply rooted in the mentorship and guidance he provided to countless programmers who followed in his footsteps. This section explores the fucking case studies that highlight Joy's commitment to nurturing the next generation of tech talent, illustrating his belief that knowledge should be shared freely and that the future of technology relies on the empowerment of its creators.

1. The Berkeley Unix Community: Cultivating Talent

At the University of California, Berkeley, where Joy first made his mark with the Berkeley Software Distribution (BSD), he didn't just write code; he built a fucking community. Joy fostered an environment where young programmers could thrive, encouraging collaboration and experimentation.

$$\text{Innovation} = \text{Collaboration} + \text{Experimentation} \tag{85}$$

This equation encapsulates Joy's philosophy. By providing mentorship and resources, he empowered students to explore their ideas, leading to a slew of innovations that would later influence the broader open-source movement. For instance, Joy worked closely with students like Mike Karels and Kirk McKusick, who would go on to be key figures in the BSD community. Their collaboration resulted in significant advancements in networking and file system technologies.

2. The Birth of Open-Source Projects: A Legacy of Sharing

Joy's influence didn't stop at Berkeley. He became a pivotal figure in the early open-source movement, advocating for the idea that software should be freely available. His mentorship extended to guiding developers in understanding the importance of open-source philosophy.

One notable example is the formation of the Free Software Foundation (FSF) and the GNU Project, where Joy's insights helped shape the discussions around software freedom. His belief that "software is like air; it should be free" resonated with many young developers who would later become leaders in the open-source community.

3. Inspiring Future Leaders at Sun Microsystems

During his tenure at Sun Microsystems, Joy didn't just focus on product development; he also took the time to mentor young engineers. He understood that the future of the company depended on cultivating a new generation of innovators. His open-door policy allowed junior engineers to approach him with ideas, questions, and even frustrations.

One case study involves a young engineer named James Gosling, who would later create the Java programming language. Joy recognized Gosling's potential and provided him with the freedom to explore his ideas, ultimately leading to the development of Java. Joy's mentorship was characterized by the following principles:

- **Encouragement of Risk-Taking:** Joy urged young engineers to take risks in their projects, reinforcing that failure was a part of the innovation process.

- **Open Dialogue:** He fostered an environment where questions were welcomed, ensuring that knowledge was shared and that no one felt intimidated by the complexity of tech.

- **Visionary Thinking:** Joy taught the importance of looking beyond immediate challenges and considering the long-term implications of technology.

4. Mentoring Through Writing and Speaking Engagements

Beyond direct mentorship, Joy also shared his knowledge through writing and public speaking. His papers, such as "The Future of Computing," not only laid out his vision for technology but also served as educational resources for aspiring programmers. In these works, he discussed theoretical aspects of programming and software design, providing frameworks that young developers could apply to their own work.

For example, Joy introduced the concept of "the network is the computer," which inspired a generation to think about distributed systems and the internet in new ways. This phrase became a rallying cry for many who would later contribute to the development of cloud computing and web technologies.

5. The Joy of Giving Back: Philanthropy and Education

In his later years, Joy has continued to mentor through philanthropic efforts, funding educational programs aimed at teaching programming to underprivileged youth. His initiatives, such as scholarships and coding boot camps, reflect his belief in the transformative power of technology education.

Joy's contributions to mentorship can be summarized with the following equation:

$$\text{Future Innovators} = \text{Mentorship} + \text{Access to Resources} + \text{Community Support} \tag{86}$$

This equation emphasizes that the next generation of programmers will thrive only if they receive proper mentorship, access to resources, and a supportive community.

Conclusion: The Lasting Impact of Joy's Mentorship

Bill Joy's mentorship has left an indelible mark on the tech industry. By investing time and energy into the development of future programmers, he ensured that his legacy would continue through the innovations and contributions of those he inspired. As we look to the future, it's clear that the principles of collaboration, open-source philosophy, and a commitment to education that Joy championed will remain vital in shaping the next fucking generation of tech leaders.

How Bill Joy Continues to Fucking Influence the Future of Computing and Technological Fucking Innovation

Bill Joy, a name that resonates through the annals of computing history, is not just a relic of the past; his influence is a fucking guiding light for the future of technology. Even decades after his groundbreaking contributions, Joy's philosophy and innovations continue to shape the landscape of computing in profound ways. This section delves into the enduring impact of Joy's vision, examining how his principles and inventions inform contemporary technological developments.

The Enduring Legacy of Open-Source Philosophy

At the heart of Bill Joy's influence is his unwavering commitment to the open-source philosophy. Joy's work on the Berkeley Software Distribution (BSD) laid the groundwork for a movement that transcends boundaries and empowers developers worldwide. The fundamental belief that software should be free and accessible has catalyzed an explosion of innovation across the globe.

The open-source model has led to the rise of collaborative platforms such as GitHub, where millions of developers contribute to projects that drive technological advancement. This collaborative spirit echoes Joy's ethos, demonstrating that sharing knowledge fosters creativity and innovation.

$$\text{Innovation} = \sum_{i=1}^{n} \text{Collaboration}_i \qquad (87)$$

This equation illustrates that innovation is a cumulative result of collaborative efforts, a principle Joy championed throughout his career. The success of projects like Linux and Apache can be traced back to the seeds planted by Joy's advocacy for open-source software.

Inspiration for New Programming Languages

Joy's role as the architect of the Java programming language has had a lasting impact on the development of new languages and frameworks. Java's "write once, run anywhere" philosophy has inspired a generation of developers to create languages that prioritize portability and ease of use.

For instance, modern languages like Kotlin and Swift have drawn upon the principles established by Java, emphasizing developer productivity and cross-platform compatibility. The influence of Joy's vision is evident in the design choices and community-driven development of these languages.

$$\text{Portability} \propto \text{Ease of Use} + \text{Community Support} \qquad (88)$$

This equation suggests that the portability of programming languages is directly proportional to their ease of use and the support they receive from the developer community, both of which are hallmarks of Joy's contributions.

Advancements in Networking and Distributed Systems

Bill Joy's innovations in networking, particularly through BSD, have set the stage for the modern internet. The TCP/IP stack, which underpins the internet, was significantly enhanced by BSD's networking capabilities. This foundation has facilitated the rise of cloud computing and distributed systems, which are now integral to everyday technology.

Joy's foresight in networking has influenced the architecture of contemporary systems such as microservices and serverless computing. These paradigms rely on principles established by Joy, emphasizing modularity, scalability, and resilience.

$$\text{Scalability} = \frac{\text{System Load}}{\text{Resource Allocation}} \qquad (89)$$

This equation demonstrates that scalability in distributed systems is determined by the relationship between system load and resource allocation, concepts that Joy's work helped to define.

Mentorship and Thought Leadership

Beyond his technical contributions, Bill Joy has played a vital role in mentoring the next generation of programmers and technologists. His insights into the future of computing and technological innovation have inspired countless individuals to pursue careers in technology. Joy's ability to articulate complex ideas in an accessible manner has made him a sought-after speaker and thought leader.

Joy's emphasis on the importance of ethics in technology continues to resonate in today's discussions about artificial intelligence, data privacy, and the societal impact of technology. His advocacy for responsible innovation serves as a reminder that with great power comes great responsibility.

$$\text{Ethical Innovation} = \text{Responsibility} + \text{Transparency} \qquad (90)$$

This equation highlights the necessity of ethical considerations in the innovation process, a principle that Joy embodies and advocates for.

The Future of Computing: Joy's Vision in Action

As we look to the future, Bill Joy's influence remains a driving force in the evolution of technology. His visionary ideas about the potential of computing continue to inspire research and development in areas such as artificial intelligence, quantum computing, and the Internet of Things (IoT).

Joy's predictions about the exponential growth of technology and its implications for society are more relevant than ever. His assertion that "the future is already here — it's just not very evenly distributed" serves as a reminder of the disparities that exist in technology access and innovation.

$$\text{Future Impact} = \text{Innovation} \times \text{Equity} \tag{91}$$

This equation suggests that the impact of future technological advancements will depend on the level of equity in access and opportunity, a concept that Joy has long championed.

In conclusion, Bill Joy's fucking influence on the future of computing and technological innovation is undeniable. From his foundational work in open-source software to his visionary insights into programming languages and networking, Joy's legacy continues to shape the trajectory of technology. As we navigate the complexities of the digital age, Joy's principles and philosophies will undoubtedly guide the next generation of innovators toward a future where technology serves as a force for good.

The Future of Fucking Computing: Will Bill Joy's Fucking Legacy Continue to Shape the Fucking World for Decades to Come?

Bill Joy's contributions to the field of computing have left an indelible mark on technology that continues to resonate across the industry. As we look towards the future of computing, it is essential to consider how Joy's philosophies and innovations may influence upcoming generations of technology and its practitioners. The following discussion outlines key areas where Joy's legacy is likely to persist, alongside the challenges and opportunities that lie ahead.

The Open-Source Movement: A Lasting Influence

One of Joy's most significant contributions is his staunch advocacy for open-source software. His belief that software should be free and accessible has laid the groundwork for a thriving open-source ecosystem. This philosophy is encapsulated in the famous quote, "Good programmers know what to write. Great programmers know what to rewrite."

In the future, as artificial intelligence (AI) and machine learning (ML) continue to evolve, the open-source movement will play a crucial role in democratizing access to these technologies. For instance, frameworks like TensorFlow and PyTorch are open-source, allowing developers worldwide to collaborate and innovate without the constraints of proprietary software. This collaborative spirit mirrors Joy's vision and ensures that the tools of the future remain accessible to all.

The Evolution of Programming Languages

Joy's role in the creation of the Java programming language has had a profound impact on software development. Java's "write once, run anywhere" capability revolutionized how applications are built and deployed. As we move forward, programming languages will continue to evolve, but the principles established by Joy will remain pivotal.

Emerging languages like Rust and Go are already adopting aspects of Joy's vision for simplicity, efficiency, and safety in programming. For example, Rust's ownership model addresses memory safety without a garbage collector, a concept that aligns with Joy's emphasis on robust software design. As new languages emerge, they will build upon the foundation laid by Joy, ensuring that his influence persists in the programming community.

The Challenges of Technological Advancement

Despite the positive trajectory of Joy's legacy, the future of computing is not without challenges. The rapid pace of technological advancement raises ethical concerns regarding privacy, security, and the digital divide. Joy himself warned of the potential consequences of unchecked technological growth, famously stating, "The future is not what it used to be."

As we navigate these challenges, Joy's emphasis on responsible innovation will be more relevant than ever. Developers and technologists must adopt a holistic view of their creations, considering not only the technical specifications but also the societal implications. This perspective is essential to ensure that technology serves humanity rather than undermines it.

The Role of Education and Mentorship

Joy's commitment to mentorship has inspired countless programmers to pursue careers in technology. As the industry evolves, the need for skilled professionals will only grow. Educational institutions must adapt to this demand by incorporating Joy's principles into their curricula.

For instance, project-based learning, which emphasizes real-world problem-solving, can cultivate the next generation of innovators. By fostering a culture of collaboration and creativity, educational programs can ensure that Joy's legacy continues to thrive. Moreover, initiatives that promote diversity in tech will be crucial in broadening the pool of talent and perspectives, further enriching the field.

Conclusion: A Legacy of Innovation and Responsibility

In summary, Bill Joy's legacy is far from static; it is a dynamic force that will continue to shape the future of computing for decades to come. As open-source software flourishes, programming languages evolve, and the industry confronts ethical dilemmas, the principles espoused by Joy will guide technologists toward responsible innovation. By embracing his vision, future generations can honor his contributions while forging a path that reflects the complexities of our modern world.

Ultimately, the question is not whether Joy's legacy will shape the future of computing, but how effectively we, as a community, can harness it to create a better, more equitable technological landscape. In the spirit of Joy's relentless pursuit of excellence, let us strive to ensure that the future of computing is not only innovative but also responsible and inclusive. The journey ahead may be fraught with challenges, but with Joy's guiding light, we can navigate the complexities of tomorrow's technology with confidence and purpose.

Index

-effectiveness, 11

ability, 3, 11, 30, 32, 39, 60, 61, 63, 70, 71, 85, 98, 107, 112
abstraction, 6, 7, 57, 62, 82
academia, 16, 94, 107
access, 1, 6, 8, 9, 11, 24, 25, 28, 29, 31, 32, 47, 55, 63, 110, 113
accessibility, 30, 86
accountability, 12, 73
achievement, 63
acknowledgment, 34
act, 72
adapt, 8, 10, 11, 65, 107
adaptability, 61, 64, 83, 90, 107
addition, 46, 64
administration, 20
adoption, 8, 17, 26, 61, 62, 70, 82
advancement, 8, 18, 50, 64, 87, 111
adversity, 17
advocacy, 12, 13, 22, 29, 30, 86, 90, 111, 112
advocate, 8, 28, 53, 87
age, 3, 32, 65, 87, 113
allocation, 18, 112
alternative, 1, 21, 29
ambition, 108
application, 59, 61, 70, 83

approach, 6, 9, 16, 28, 35, 42, 51, 63, 71, 73, 75, 78, 95, 106
architect, 6, 8
architecture, 26, 27, 42, 46, 47, 59–61, 65, 112
argument, 10
art, 30
aspect, 34, 60
asset, 9
atmosphere, 95
authentication, 8
automation, 19
availability, 60

backbone, 36
background, 32
backlash, 91
balance, 32, 50, 62, 72, 73, 91, 94, 98, 108
balancing, 2, 51, 72, 75, 99, 107
ball, 64
barrier, 28
base, 19
battle, 20, 22, 28, 30
beacon, 3, 65
bedrock, 16
being, 62, 94, 95, 99, 103, 108
belief, 9, 22, 27, 28, 30–32, 94, 110

Berkeley, 3, 106
bias, 12, 88
Bill Joy, 3, 6, 8, 18, 19, 28, 30, 46, 50, 56, 61, 64, 84, 85, 87, 93, 97, 105, 112
Bill Joy's, 1, 3, 8, 13, 17, 22, 27, 30, 32, 35, 43, 58, 65, 71, 84, 86, 90, 99, 108, 113
blend, 17
boot, 110
boundary, 99
box, 70
break, 8, 45, 98
breakthrough, 16, 19
breathing, 9, 64
breeding, 19, 82
brilliance, 106
browser, 63
building, 24, 31, 65
burnout, 96, 107
business, 2, 9, 50, 51, 107
bytecode, 7, 57, 62–64

capability, 8
care, 108
career, 1, 32, 49, 87, 93, 96, 106, 108, 111
case, 10, 16, 29, 35, 36, 59, 61, 84
cause, 38
century, 20, 28
challenge, 2, 24, 26, 29, 51, 62, 70, 72, 91, 94, 97, 99, 107
champion, 22, 32, 90
change, 9, 22, 70, 86
changer, 59
chaos, 97
choice, 24, 25, 27, 65, 85
client, 47, 83
cloud, 8, 11, 13, 27, 38, 61, 65

co, 41
code, 3, 6, 7, 9, 10, 19, 20, 28–32, 48, 53, 55, 62, 63, 82
codebase, 31, 35
coding, 32, 86, 110
cohesion, 71
collaboration, 3, 8–10, 13, 16, 17, 19, 20, 22, 26–30, 32, 34, 38, 45, 49, 56, 71, 77, 81, 82, 86, 87, 95, 98, 106, 108, 109
collector, 114
combination, 6, 71, 105
command, 85
commercialization, 39
commitment, 27, 31, 32, 43, 49, 90, 106
communication, 24, 72, 83
community, 3, 8–10, 13, 16, 17, 19, 20, 26–28, 30–32, 34, 36, 39, 49, 56, 58, 64, 65, 82, 86, 98, 107, 109–112, 114
company, 41–43, 46, 50, 72
compatibility, 46, 62, 111
competition, 2, 42, 72
competitor, 20, 70
compilation, 7, 62
compiler, 19
complexity, 26, 60, 80
computing, 1, 3, 6, 8, 9, 11, 13, 17, 25, 27, 28, 30, 35, 36, 38, 42, 43, 49, 58, 60, 61, 70, 87, 89, 93, 107, 112, 113
concept, 16, 18, 58, 113, 114
conclusion, 3, 13, 17, 27, 30, 32, 35, 43, 65, 84, 86, 99, 113
connection, 99
connectivity, 8
consumption, 89

Index

container, 60
containerization, 26, 38
contemporary, 112
contender, 16
contrast, 31
control, 20, 29, 72, 82
convenience, 56
cooperation, 34
core, 9, 30
corner, 86
cornerstone, 2, 5, 6, 18, 22, 24, 36,
    61, 87, 106
cost, 11, 97, 107, 108
course, 6
creation, 6, 35, 36, 47, 63, 85, 106
creativity, 3, 9, 16, 45, 71, 75, 94, 111
creator, 10, 31, 34, 90
critic, 32
criticism, 62
cross, 35, 111
cry, 27, 29
crystal, 64
culture, 2, 3, 16, 20, 29–32, 34, 49,
    72, 77, 87, 103, 106
curiosity, 22
curve, 26
cybersecurity, 10
cycle, 96, 99

data, 8, 10, 24, 25, 47, 64, 65, 91,
    112
database, 8
decision, 28, 91, 107
dedication, 31
defense, 64
delegation, 99
demand, 72
departure, 9, 34, 42
dependency, 60

deployment, 59
descendant, 31
design, 13, 17, 34, 64, 85, 111, 114
determination, 3, 17
developer, 111, 112
development, 5, 6, 8, 10, 12, 16, 17,
    19, 22, 27, 31, 32, 34–36,
    45–47, 49, 53, 55, 58–61,
    63, 65, 70, 73, 75, 82, 83,
    85–88, 90, 94, 107, 111
device, 13, 48, 61, 75, 94
disk, 18
disparity, 26
distribution, 9, 20, 34
documentation, 19, 20, 31
domain, 29
dream, 13, 58, 72
drive, 2, 17, 22, 50, 86, 93, 94, 97,
    99, 111
duality, 38, 50
dynamic, 8, 94

ease, 24, 82, 112
ecosystem, 8, 10, 19, 22, 28, 39, 49,
    56, 64, 107
edge, 35
editing, 85
editor, 16, 19, 85
education, 31, 32, 110
effectiveness, 11, 99
efficiency, 11, 16, 17, 25, 42, 82, 85,
    114
effort, 9, 21, 106
Elon Musk, 78
emergence, 10, 36, 83
emphasis, 20, 82, 86, 112, 114
empowerment, 71
endeavor, 31, 106
energy, 89

engagement, 8, 26, 82
enterprise, 8, 59–61, 64, 70
entity, 9
entry, 28, 32
environment, 7, 17, 19, 27, 28, 42, 48, 55, 57, 63, 71, 73, 77, 90, 94, 98, 108
equation, 3, 6, 7, 10, 11, 13, 22, 24, 26, 39, 50, 57, 77, 80, 82, 87, 88, 97, 101, 108, 110–113
equilibrium, 97
equity, 113
era, 28
essence, 6
establishment, 3
ethos, 3, 8, 29, 111
evolution, 3, 12, 13, 46, 64, 84, 86, 87
example, 10, 29, 30, 36, 48, 78, 91, 114
excellence, 3, 17
exception, 97
execution, 6, 48, 62, 72, 73
existence, 98
expansion, 12
expectation, 96
expense, 94, 99
experience, 42, 60, 99, 106
experiment, 77
experimentation, 51, 106
expertise, 43, 107
extensibility, 85
extension, 18

fabric, 1, 3, 30
face, 8, 17, 64
fact, 58
failure, 106
fairness, 12
family, 94, 99
fault, 60
favorite, 85
fear, 16, 22, 29
feature, 55, 63
fight, 22, 29, 30
figurehead, 96
file, 19, 27, 35, 47, 109
flexibility, 11, 16, 60, 62, 107
flow, 72
focus, 6, 24, 83, 94, 103
following, 6, 26, 48, 50, 77, 80–82, 88, 110
footnote, 6
force, 3, 58, 107, 113
forefront, 50, 65
foresight, 11, 13, 58, 81, 87, 90, 91, 107, 112
form, 30, 62
foster, 3, 8, 78, 90, 106
fostering, 17, 26, 31, 36, 56, 72, 73, 77, 82, 87, 90, 94, 98, 103, 106–108
foundation, 5, 8, 13, 16, 17, 26, 27, 34, 35, 46, 114
founding, 43, 94
fragmentation, 62
framework, 34, 51, 80, 84, 86, 90
freedom, 72
friendliness, 26
fucking, 6, 8, 25, 30, 32, 35, 36, 50, 61, 64, 65, 72, 73, 93, 94, 105, 106, 108, 113
fulfillment, 99
function, 26, 57
functionality, 21, 33
funding, 110
funnel, 72

Index

future, 3, 6, 8, 10, 11, 13, 17, 25, 27, 30, 32, 39, 43, 61, 63–65, 78, 84, 106–108, 112, 113

gain, 26
game, 59
garbage, 114
gcc, 19
generation, 8, 9, 22, 29, 31, 34, 35, 71, 86, 108, 110, 112, 113
genius, 3, 8, 93, 105
globe, 30, 36, 65, 88
go, 17, 25, 109
goal, 61, 107
good, 113
grade, 65
grip, 28
ground, 19, 82
groundbreaking, 1, 2, 8, 10, 18, 30, 45, 46, 50, 51, 63, 71, 77, 96, 97, 106, 107
groundwork, 2, 3, 9, 21, 34, 35, 42, 47, 63, 65, 70, 82, 84, 87, 107
group, 106
growth, 19, 28, 32, 71, 80, 83, 86, 87
guilt, 99

hardware, 6, 8, 56, 85
head, 17, 24, 56, 71
health, 103
heart, 22, 72
history, 6, 43
human, 88, 99
humanity, 22

idea, 9, 22, 30, 72
ideal, 32
imagination, 65
imbalance, 99

impact, 1, 3, 5, 9, 10, 16, 17, 24, 29, 31, 35, 36, 46, 47, 49, 58, 59, 61, 84, 85, 88, 91, 101, 112, 113
implementation, 18, 62
importance, 3, 8, 19, 24, 26, 31, 32, 49, 55, 72, 73, 81, 87, 94, 95, 103, 107, 112
improvement, 77
in, 3, 5–13, 16–18, 20, 22, 24–32, 34–36, 42, 43, 46–50, 53, 55, 58–65, 70–73, 75, 80, 82, 83, 85–88, 91, 93, 94, 96, 106–114
inclusivity, 12, 13, 32
independence, 48, 61–63
individual, 3, 103
industry, 3, 8, 9, 16, 28, 30, 32, 42, 49, 51, 55, 58, 71, 84, 86, 105–108
influence, 3, 6, 8, 13, 17, 26, 27, 32, 34, 35, 58, 61, 71, 82, 84–87, 108, 111, 113, 114
ingenuity, 61
injection, 60
innovation, 1–3, 7, 9, 10, 13, 16–20, 22, 24, 27–32, 34, 39, 43, 45, 49–51, 63, 65, 71–73, 75, 77, 78, 83, 85, 86, 88, 90, 91, 93, 94, 97, 99, 103, 106–108, 111–113
inspiration, 8, 34, 99
installation, 20
instance, 16, 26, 31, 47, 77, 94, 99, 108, 111
integration, 16, 19, 61, 87
integrity, 64
intellect, 1
intelligence, 8, 87, 88, 112

interconnection, 86
interface, 24, 42
intermediary, 6
internet, 11, 43, 55, 94, 107
interoperability, 27, 86
interplay, 2
introduction, 16, 60, 61, 64
involvement, 31, 49
isolation, 16, 99, 106

Java, 6, 8, 48, 55–65, 70, 71, 73, 75, 82, 85, 86, 94, 96, 107, 111
journey, 1, 3, 17, 42, 56, 58, 61, 97, 99, 108
Joy, 1–3, 5, 6, 8–10, 12, 13, 16, 17, 19, 22, 25–32, 34–36, 38, 41–43, 46–51, 55–58, 64, 65, 70–73, 75, 82–86, 91, 93–99, 106–108, 110–114
JVM, 6, 48, 62, 63

kernel, 36
Kirk McKusick, 108
knowledge, 8, 17, 19, 21, 22, 30–32, 49, 53, 83, 86, 107, 111
Kotlin, 111

lab, 25
lack, 28
landmark, 63
landscape, 2, 3, 8–10, 20, 25, 26, 29, 31, 32, 35, 38, 43, 46, 58, 61, 63, 64, 70, 72, 86, 87, 93, 97, 106–108
language, 6, 8, 47, 48, 55–58, 61, 64, 65, 70, 73, 75, 82, 85, 86, 94, 107
latency, 24
layer, 6, 7, 57, 62
lead, 9, 36, 86, 87, 106, 107

leader, 49, 71, 112
leadership, 2, 17, 35, 50, 70–73, 103
learning, 26, 32, 88
legacy, 3, 6, 8, 13, 17, 22, 26, 27, 30, 32, 34–36, 43, 53, 58, 65, 71, 86, 99, 106, 113
leisure, 98
lesson, 106–108
level, 63, 72, 82, 113
leverage, 27, 39, 42, 65
licensing, 8, 34, 35
life, 73, 87, 93, 94, 97–99, 108
light, 13, 63
like, 2, 5, 9, 18, 20, 22, 27, 28, 30, 32, 36, 38, 49, 53, 61, 64, 65, 77, 78, 82, 83, 88, 90, 96, 101, 108, 111, 114
lineage, 34
Linus Torvalds, 10, 29, 31, 34, 36, 90
Linux, 26, 34–36, 87, 90
living, 9, 64
load, 112
logic, 83
lot, 9

machine, 2, 62, 88
making, 9, 24, 43, 56, 60, 64, 91, 107
man, 13
management, 57
manager, 55
manner, 112
mantra, 30
mark, 9, 30, 35, 64, 84, 108
market, 2, 42, 107
Marshall Kirk McKusick, 16
means, 28
meeting, 51
memory, 16, 18, 114
mentality, 1, 9, 28–30, 32

mentor, 110
mentoring, 112
mentorship, 108, 110
methodology, 16
mettle, 61
microprocessor, 42
Mike Karels, 16, 108
mind, 12
mindfulness, 99
mindset, 22, 77
mission, 17
mitigation, 88
mobile, 8, 58
model, 8, 10, 20, 22, 27, 28, 30, 31, 34, 35, 47, 55, 63, 72, 82, 83, 111, 114
modification, 28, 86
modularity, 27, 60, 112
moment, 6, 43
momentum, 32
move, 84
movement, 10, 21, 22, 30, 32, 34, 87, 107, 108
music, 9
myriad, 16

name, 8, 28, 41
narrative, 3
nature, 10, 28, 31
necessity, 32, 60, 106, 112
need, 2, 36, 39, 47, 50, 57, 84, 85, 91, 95, 108
NetBSD, 5, 27
network, 17, 24, 80, 83
networking, 1, 6, 24, 27, 34, 35, 42, 43, 83, 84, 109, 112, 113
notion, 9, 22, 27

on, 1, 3, 6, 8–10, 13, 16, 17, 20, 24, 26–28, 30, 32, 34–36, 39, 42, 46–49, 51, 56–58, 61, 62, 64, 71, 75, 82–87, 93, 94, 96, 99, 103, 108, 109, 112–114
one, 1, 3, 6, 8, 20, 27, 28, 43, 62, 64, 85
openness, 22, 32, 103
operating, 2, 5, 6, 10, 17, 18, 24–27, 29, 31, 34–36, 46, 58, 70, 82, 84, 106
opportunity, 113
organization, 45
other, 18, 25, 34, 42, 63
overhead, 62
ownership, 75, 114

pace, 51
paradigm, 20, 42
park, 61
passion, 16
past, 65
path, 1, 47
people, 32, 65
perception, 26
perfection, 2, 73, 93
performance, 18, 24, 25, 27, 46, 48, 49, 57, 62
perspective, 22, 30, 78
philanthropic, 110
philosophy, 3, 6, 8–10, 27–33, 49, 53, 72, 77, 90, 106, 108
pioneer, 106
place, 6, 8, 65
platform, 6, 48, 61–63, 70, 71, 73, 82, 107, 111
play, 64
playground, 36
plethora, 61

pollination, 35
popularity, 27, 62
popularization, 85
portability, 7, 27, 58, 62, 65, 85, 112
portfolio, 51
position, 20, 60
potential, 10, 16, 20, 28, 48, 55, 73, 99
power, 3, 17, 21, 29, 30, 32, 65, 89, 106, 108, 110, 112
powerhouse, 17, 25, 50
practice, 8
pragmatism, 106
precedent, 33
pressure, 94, 96, 98, 107
principle, 3, 8, 30, 62, 90, 111, 112
privacy, 10, 12, 91, 112
problem, 16, 46, 49
process, 7, 10, 62, 72, 112
processing, 65
prodigy, 6, 97
product, 31, 45, 94
production, 65
productivity, 85, 111
professional, 97, 99, 107
profit, 22, 28
profitability, 22
program, 6, 48
programming, 3, 6, 8, 13, 19, 22, 24, 30–32, 47, 56, 57, 60, 61, 63, 64, 70, 73, 82–87, 94, 97, 110, 112–114
progress, 9, 22, 28, 90
project, 1, 31, 36, 47, 73, 94, 99
proliferation, 82
promise, 58
property, 9, 32
prophet, 87
prototyping, 16

prowess, 6, 17, 46, 94
public, 29, 96
pursuit, 2, 3, 17, 50, 73, 94, 97, 99
push, 2, 17, 42, 58, 70, 71, 84

quest, 93
quo, 35

rate, 88
reach, 21
realm, 53, 58, 59, 64
redistribution, 28
relationship, 57, 80, 82, 88, 89, 112
release, 21, 51
relevance, 8, 26, 27, 38, 61
reliability, 25, 27
reminder, 3, 32, 71, 91, 107, 112
reputation, 71
research, 17, 87, 88
resilience, 71, 112
resistance, 22, 31
resource, 16, 30, 57, 112
response, 60, 107
responsibility, 91, 112
responsiveness, 18
restriction, 22
result, 25, 36, 70, 71, 106, 111
retribution, 22
revenue, 50
revolution, 6, 36, 43, 50
revolutionary, 21, 28, 42, 50, 59, 61, 62, 84
richness, 99
right, 71
rise, 5, 8, 10, 11, 27, 29, 31, 32, 38, 53, 61, 63, 65, 86, 88, 90, 111
risk, 3, 62, 63
road, 2

roadmap, 106
robustness, 8, 26
role, 6, 59, 61, 64, 73, 85, 112
runtime, 57
Rust, 114

s, 1–3, 6, 8–13, 16, 17, 19, 22,
    25–32, 34–36, 41, 43,
    47–49, 58, 60–62, 64, 65,
    70–73, 82–86, 90, 91, 93,
    94, 98, 99, 106–108,
    110–114
safety, 114
sandbox, 7, 63
sandboxing, 64
scalability, 11, 16, 18, 27, 112
scripting, 85
secrecy, 20
section, 1, 6, 8, 28, 35, 46, 50, 59,
    84, 93
security, 7, 12, 13, 16, 26–28, 35, 48,
    55, 57, 63–65, 71
seek, 65
self, 108
sense, 36, 73, 75, 98
server, 10, 27, 30, 36, 42, 47, 83
serverless, 112
service, 27
set, 2, 6, 22, 33, 36, 50, 55, 62
setback, 106
shape, 13, 35, 64, 113
sharing, 9, 19, 20, 31, 32, 34, 49, 56,
    86, 87, 107, 111
shift, 11, 36, 95
significance, 26, 80
Silicon Valley, 94, 98
simplicity, 114
skepticism, 55
skill, 30

slew, 108
snippet, 48
society, 12
software, 1–3, 5, 6, 8–10, 13,
    19–22, 25, 27–32, 34, 35,
    38, 43, 49, 53, 56, 58, 59,
    61, 65, 75, 80, 85–88, 90,
    106, 107, 111, 113, 114
Solaris, 46
solution, 10, 47
solving, 16, 49
source, 3, 5, 6, 8–10, 12, 13, 17, 19,
    21, 22, 26–36, 38, 39, 43,
    49, 53, 56, 62, 82, 86–88,
    90, 106–108, 111, 113
space, 16, 18, 36
speaker, 112
specific, 56, 86
speed, 24, 25
spirit, 1, 8, 17, 27, 31, 32, 36, 46, 111
stability, 16
stage, 2, 6, 43
stakeholder, 72
stance, 32
stand, 65
standard, 26, 91
staple, 16, 49, 85
statement, 1
status, 35
step, 62
stone, 106
storage, 25
story, 3
strain, 107
stranger, 93
strategy, 72
streaming, 60
stress, 94, 96, 99
stronghold, 42

structure, 72
struggle, 29
style, 2, 17, 71, 73
success, 2, 3, 5, 10, 16, 19, 30, 31, 43, 50, 71, 99, 106, 107, 111
summary, 8, 58
support, 20, 26, 49, 95, 103, 112
surveillance, 91
sustainability, 38, 108
Swift, 111
synergy, 77
system, 2, 5, 10, 16–20, 25–27, 29, 31, 36, 46, 48, 58, 63, 82, 85, 109, 112

t, 9
taking, 3
tale, 1, 99, 108
task, 107
teaching, 31, 110
team, 1, 2, 16–19, 24, 35, 42, 46, 48, 57, 61, 62, 70, 71, 73, 75, 86, 94, 95, 98, 103
teamwork, 45
tech, 1–3, 8–10, 22, 27, 28, 30, 32, 43, 50, 51, 53, 58, 61, 71, 72, 84, 86, 91, 93, 96, 97, 105–108
technology, 1–3, 6, 8, 13, 17, 22, 25, 30–32, 35, 43, 46, 49, 50, 71, 78, 84, 86, 87, 91, 99, 106, 107, 110, 112, 113
tension, 17, 72, 94
tenure, 46, 50, 73
term, 10, 51, 78, 108
test, 87
testament, 3, 17, 27, 29, 53, 58, 65, 108
testing, 16

text, 16, 19, 85
thing, 28
thinking, 17, 27, 43, 71, 84, 86, 94
thought, 88, 112
threat, 9, 22, 99
thrive, 5, 8, 38, 56, 72, 110
throughput, 24
time, 2, 9, 34, 42, 51, 63, 70, 87, 88, 98, 105
today, 5, 8, 24, 27, 30, 32, 47, 49, 84, 85, 106, 112
tolerance, 60
toll, 93
tool, 17, 19, 60, 85
toolkit, 60
Torvalds, 34
traction, 26, 55
trade, 28
trajectory, 43, 84, 87, 113
transformation, 7
transition, 2, 107
transmission, 24
transparency, 9, 10, 12, 13, 28, 30, 38, 49, 82
turn, 71

underpinning, 6
understanding, 72, 107
usability, 6, 46
use, 2, 18, 24, 63, 64, 84, 112
user, 8, 10, 17, 19, 26, 34, 42, 47, 60, 83, 85
utilization, 16

variety, 46
verification, 63, 64
versatility, 8, 48
vision, 2, 3, 6, 8, 10, 12, 13, 22, 25–28, 30, 32, 35, 47,

56–58, 61, 65, 73, 75, 80, 84–86, 107, 108, 111, 114
visionary, 8, 17, 27, 30, 50, 71, 78, 84, 86, 90, 91, 97, 113

walk, 61
wave, 31
way, 30, 32, 34, 36, 43, 56, 61, 84, 87, 108
web, 6–8, 10, 30, 36, 55, 59–61, 63, 70, 83, 86, 88
well, 35, 94, 95, 99, 103, 108
whole, 30

willingness, 106, 107
work, 1, 3, 8, 10, 22, 29, 34, 36, 62, 84, 87, 94, 95, 97–99, 107, 108, 112, 113
workstation, 2, 42, 47
world, 1, 3, 6, 9, 10, 13, 21, 22, 27, 29–32, 35, 53, 56, 64, 65, 84, 86, 93, 94, 96, 99, 107, 108
writing, 6

youth, 110

Milton Keynes UK
Ingram Content Group UK Ltd.
UKHW020319021124
450424UK00013B/1329